THE MAKING PROCESS OF GOD'S LEADERS

THE MAKING PROCESS OF GOD'S LEADERS

A METAMORPHIC BREAKDOWN OF TRUE LEADERSHIP

DR. JOHN A. TETSOLA

Table of Contents

Acknowledgments

My sincere thanks and gratitude to those who have helped make this book a success through prayer and fasting. A special thanks goes to the following for their financial support:

Carrie Anderson
Fannie Guest
Leroy Lawrence
Josephine Motley
Joy Wilson

Dedication

This book is dedicated to the entire Body of Christ— to God's generals, present leaders, young leaders, to those who are still in the making and to all of God's people on the cutting edge of His move.

Preface

Where does the Church stand in today's society of confusion and hopelessness? The Church stands where *its leaders* lead Her to stand. We need a new breed of leaders today who will "rise to the challenge" and "champion" the cause of Christ in this dark hour. Not only is the *world* groping for *true* leadership, so also, is the *Church.* The cry is, "Give us leaders. Real leaders. True leaders. Honest leaders. Strong leaders. Consistent leaders. Leaders with Biblical values. Leaders with conviction. Someone, please give us leaders!"

The Church needs strong leaders like never before. Our task today is to meet this need by raising solid Biblical leaders who will boldly minister to those who have abandoned God's ordinances. We need champions who dare to proclaim the unadulterated Word of God in the face of humanistic and ungodly philosophy that tarnishes our 20th Century society.

God has *never* been known to promote giftings. He only promotes character. This kind of character is not developed overnight. This kind of character is developed during the seasons of preparation.

It is during this season of preparation, within the midst of "God's factory" that *true* leaders are made. This is the making process of God's leaders.

Dr. John A. Tetsola

CHAPTER 1

THE LEADERSHIP PROCESS

For too long, the Church has had problems understanding God's leadership process. Many cannot understand why God makes servants first, and then servants become leaders. We must understand that the principles of God's Kingdom or spiritual laws differ from the principles of this world. This world will tell you that, to be rich, you must amass more wealth. God's principle or law says, "Give and it shall be given back to you." God's principles are opposite man's principles. The Church must understand God's leadership process.

Power Struggle

> **And there was also strife among them, which of them should be accounted the greatest.**
>
> **And he said unto them, The kings of the Gentiles exercise leadership over them; and they that exercise authorities upon them are called benefactors.**
>
> **But ye shall not be so: but he that is greatest among you, let him be as the younger, and he that is chief, as he that doth serve.**

> **For whether is greater, he that sitteth at meat, or he that serveth? is not he that sitteth at meat? But I am among you as he that serveth.**
>
> **Luke 22:24-27**

The disciples here were at it again. On the very eve of Christ's crucifixion, they were arguing and there was strife among them, as to which of them should be accounted the greatest.

> **And he said unto them, "The kings of the Gentiles exercise lordship over them; and they that exercise authorities upon them are called benefactors."**
>
> **But ye shall not be so: but he that is greatest among you, let him be as the younger; and he that is chief, as he that doth serve.**
>
> **For whether is greater, he that sitteth at meat, or he that serveth? is not he that sitteth at meat? but I am among you as he that serveth.**
>
> **Luke 22:25-27**

They might have been measuring their need for greatness based on the roles, activities and part they played in Jesus's ministry. Jesus burst their bubbles of pride and selfishness. They were expecting Jesus to inaugurate a new kingdom. However, Jesus shattered their dreams and silenced their quarreling by pointing out, "The kings of the Gentiles exercise lordship over them; and they that exercise authorities upon them are called benefactors." You are not to be like that.

The Role of Bondservants

Jesus knowing that the Father had given all things into his hands, and that he was come from God, and went to God;

He riseth from supper, and laid aside his garments; and took a towel, and girded himself.

After that he poureth water into a bason, and began to wash the disciples' feet, and to wipe them with the towel wherewith he was girded.

So after he had washed their feet, and had taken his garments, and was set down again, he said unto them, Know ye what I have done to you?

Ye call me Master and Lord: and ye say well; for so I am.

If I then, your Lord and Master, have washed your feet; ye also ought to wash one another's feet.

For I have given you an example, that ye should do as I have done to you.

John 13:3-5, 12-15, 17

Here, Jesus undertook the role of the lowest slave. It was an act of love and humility. The dusty, dirty feet of His disciples needed washing. Since there was no house slave around, Jesus performed the task. How embarrassing! I can almost visualize the dozen red faces as He knelt to wash their feet. But Jesus was showing His disciples the leadership process. Leadership does not start from the top. It starts from the bottom. This is the law of the Kingdom.

Jesus established the foundation of scriptural leadership. The essence of leadership is service. Spiritual leaders are called to serve God and His people. This is non-negotiable. Christian leaders are expected to put this into practice.

Servanthood

The Greek translation for "servant" is *diakonos.* This word appears thirty times in the New Testament, and its cognates, *diakoneo* (to minister) and *diakonia* (ministers of service), are used in seventy references. Originally, *diakonos* was translated "table waiter" or "servant."

> **But Martha was cumbered about much serving, and came to him, and said, Lord, dost thou not care that my sister hath left me to serve alone? bid her therefore that she help me.**
>
> **Luke 10:40**

> **And he came and took her by the hand, and lifted her up; and immediately the fever left her, and she ministered unto them.**
>
> **Mark 1:31**

The service rendered by Martha or Peter's mother-in-law is described as *diakonia.*

For whether is greater, he that sitteth at meat, or he that serveth? Is not he that sitteth at meat? But I am among you as he that serveth.

Luke 22:27

Jesus here described Himself as a table waiter. The emphasis is on practical service or ministry.

AND IN those days, when the number of the disciples was multiplied, there arose a murmuring of the Grecians against the Hebrews, because their widows were neglected in the daily ministration.

Then the twelve called the multitude of the disciples *unto them*, and said, It is not reason that we should leave the word of God, and serve tables.

Acts 6:1-2

This area of ministry is understood in the appointment of the seven to distribute food to the greek-speaking widows in the Jerusalem church. It does not equate leadership with privileges and authority. Functional leaders are commissioned to serve others. The only sense of privilege stems from God's gracious calling.

The Divisions Among Leaders

For it hath been declared unto me of you, my brethren, by them which are of the house of Chloe, that there are contentions among you.

> **Now this I say, that every one of you saith, I am of Paul; and I of Apollos; and I of Cephas; and I of Christ.**
>
> **I Corinthians 1:11-12**

Most Christians have a wrong view of leadership. The church at Corinth was in the same predicament. They had a wrong view of leadership. Promotion of personality cults had led to quarrels and divisions within the church. Some Christians idolized Paul. After all, he had founded their church and was a spiritual father to many of them. Another group applauded for Apollos. They were captivated by his systematic and intellectual preaching. Apollos came from the university center of Alexandria, and was a powerful apologist. The third party preferred Peter. Wasn't he the chief apostle? To them, he embodied the conservative element of the Church. Paul and Apollos were radicals by comparison. This group was eager to observe the customs and tradition, and to be ruled by the letter of the law. Then there was an extraordinary fourth party – "the Christ party." Its members were hyperspiritual. Instead of working toward unity in Christ, they made Christ a party leader. They waved His banner and made themselves out to be, by far, the best party.

> **Is Christ divided? Was Paul crucified for you? Or were ye baptized in the name of Paul?**
>
> **I Corinthians 1:13**

Do you notice how Paul dealt with this spirit? Notice how he dealt a blow to the shameful personality cults that the Corinthian church had created? Paul reminded them of their unity in Christ. Their allegiance was to Christ crucified, not to any human leaders. Paul did not stop there. His anxious desire was that the Corinthian Christians be taught to honor and relate to their leaders.

Apostolic Adjustment

> **And I, brethren, could not speak unto you as unto spiritual, but as unto carnal, *even* as unto babes in Christ.**
>
> **I have fed you with milk, and not with meat: for hitherto ye were not able *to bear it*, neither yet now are ye able.**
>
> **For ye are yet carnal: for whereas *there is* among you envying, and strife, and divisions, are ye not carnal, and walk as men?**
>
> **For while one saith, I am of Paul; and another, I *am* of Apollos, are ye not carnal?**
>
> **Who then is Paul, and who is Apollos, but ministers by whom ye believed, even as the Lord gave to every man?**
>
> **I have planted, Apollos watered; but God gave the increase.**
>
> **So then neither is he that planteth anything neither he that watereth; but God that giveth the increase.**
>
> **Now he that planteth and he that watereth are one: and every man shall receive his own reward according to his own labor.**

For we are laborers together with God: ye are God's husbandry, ***ye are*** **God's building.**

I Corinthians 3:1-9

Here Paul began to bring apostolic adjustment to the Corinthian church. Jealousy, quarreling and the promotion of personality cults are not God's order for Christian conduct. They were acting as "mere men" and not following the way of Christ. Instead of Paul saying, "Who, after all, is Apollos? And who is Paul?" He deliberately chose the neutral pronoun "what," as if to say, "what thing is Apollos or Paul?" Then, Paul gave this definitive answer: "Only servants, through whom you came to believe." They were simply the agents of their salvation, not the objects of their faith.

Paul explained the different task that God assigns to His servants. Paul planted the gospel seed. Apollos watered it. But, it was God who caused the seed to grow. The servants played their role in the Corinthian harvest, but only the Lord Himself could produce spiritual life. This process must be properly understood by the leaders God is raising and making today.

CHAPTER 2

THE FACTORY OF GOD

The birthing, training and development of true leadership involves true transformation. This transformation takes place in the "factory of God." Any leader of God's people must be manufactured from God's own factory and marketed by God Himself.

> **And Jesus, walking by the sea of Galilee, saw two brethren, Simon called Peter and Andrew his brother, casting a net into the sea: for they were fishers.**
>
> **And he saith unto them, "Follow me, and I will make you fishers of men.**
>
> **Matthew 4:18-19**

In this present move of God's Spirit, God is calling for men and women who will yield to His making process. God wants to "make" leaders that will lead churches and birth other leaders. In order to fully understand God's making process, let us look at the manufacturing process in a factory and then draw an analogy from it.

A factory is a place where goods are made with machinery. These goods or products undergo a multifaceted process before the end-product is approved, released and distributed. This process is known as manufacturing. Manufacturing literally means "to make by hand." Let's look at the food manufacturing industry. This will shed some light and open the door to the understanding of God's manufacturing process of His leaders.

Growth and Selection

The food manufacturing process includes growing and selecting raw materials, harvesting, processing, preserving, packaging, labeling and distributing. Usually, there's a group of people selected to monitor the growth of individual food items or raw material. When these items are fully developed, they are properly harvested and separated for processing. God begins His manufacturing process in us by our faithfulness in the little things. As we remain faithful and committed to the little assignments in our lives, God begins to develop gifting and then grows us in the art of leading. David is a good example. He began by taking care of his father's sheep, and out of his faithfulness God began to develop leadership qualities in him.

The Processing Step

Usually, the processing step is quite sophisticated and tedious. It is often the most critical and costly step to the manufacturer. The process may include cleaning, cutting, pureeing, dehydrating, preserving, etc. That is what God does with His leaders. He cuts away the dead branches. In the processing stage, God begins a character work in us. He begins to expose the impurity in us so that it can be dealt with.

The Packaging Step

The next step in the process is packaging and God is the Master Packager. He knows the outer casing is essential because it ensures separation and protection of the product from external, physical and environmental forces. There are almost as many packaging techniques as there are products. Various media are used to package the product, such as metal, plastic, cardboard, paper, and many other types of containers. Yet, in the packaging process, there are only three levels.

The primary level or layer is the packaging that makes direct contact with the product. It is the most intimate layer between the product and its environment. The second layer is supplemental to the primary level, and provides further protection, support and ease of handling the product and its contents. The third or tertiary layer, is the outer layer for distribution. An example is a carbonated drink in an aluminum can. The primary layer is the can itself. The secondary layer is the interconnected plastic rings that hold multiple cans together, and the tertiary layer is the cardboard carton necessary to ship and distribute the product.

Too often, Christians and leaders attempt to package themselves without submitting to every level of God's process. They fail to "sell," because they cannot make it through the physical, external and environmental influences. They reach the distribution stage damaged and below acceptable market value. God's leaders in this season will be packaged and marketed by Him alone. What God packages becomes the best product on the retailer's shelf. Allow God to package you!

Quality Assurance

Throughout the process, the Quality Assurance committee plays an important role. They constantly monitor all aspects of the process by inspecting and testing the products. Their goal is to make sure that the highest level of quality is achieved.

After careful inspection and testing, the next step is the labeling process which is done in accordance with industry standards and regulatory statutes. These are approved and established by the federal government. The labeling process is extremely important because the product must accurately reflect the manufacturer's claims (i.e. quality, quantity, weight, volume or count), along with the name and address of the manufacturer.

This illustration was given as an example of the greatest Manufacturer of all time, "Elohim" the Creator God. God's factory is called the "Factory of Time." The products released from this factory are polished, seasoned and accurate men and women who will carry out His purpose to the letter, and will serve the purpose of his or her generation. It is in the

"Factory" that the manufacturing (making by hand: God's hand) of all leaders must take place.

God begins His making process with "raw" materials. At each stage in His Factory, He works the ingredients with His own hands, investing them with His qualities, grace-given abilities, talents and anointing. The Master Packager knows when the preparation is complete and made ready to be released to the consumers – the people of God. Allow yourself to go through God's factory, for it is only in His factory that He makes us.

CHAPTER 3

THE SEASON OF PREPARATION

And let them also be tried and investigated and proved first; then, (if they turn out to be above reproach, let them serve (as deacons).

I Timothy 3:10 AMP

The growth and maturity of every leader is decided in their seasons of preparation. First of all, a leader's season of preparation involves the leader's salvation. This is where his or her ministry is planted as a seed. The next step is the leader's call, and this has to do with the ministry being birthed as a sprout. Then, the next stage is the leader's preparation, involving the testing of the ministry as a plant. The final stage is the leader's function. It is then that his or her ministry is fully matured, as a fruit-bearing tree.

Many leaders have had problems developing past the point of identifying and fulfilling their specific calling in the Lord. Some may identify their call, but then fail to prepare for their ministries. Still others receive their calling and proceed into the preparation period, but fail in the process. Unfortunately, some leaders die in the wilderness at some point in their development.

The Stages of Preparation

Listen, O isles, unto me; and hearken, ye people from far. The Lord hath called me from the womb; from the bowels of my mother hath he made mention of my name.

And he hath made my mouth like a sharp sword; in the shadow of his hand hath he hid me, and made me a polished shaft; in his quiver hath he hid me;

And said unto me, Thou *art* my servant, O Israel, in whom I will be glorified.

Isaiah 49:1-3

The prophet Isaiah gave an interesting illustration regarding these periods and stages of preparation. This will provide understanding for believers aspiring to be leaders, and even those already in leadership positions.

"The Lord Called Me from the Womb"

God's call upon the life of Isaiah was evident from his mother's womb. Before the prophet Isaiah's birth, the purpose of God for his life was determined. This specific call was also fulfilled in the life of Jesus Christ. It is also fulfilled in God's servants. God has a purpose for each of His servants. The purpose was established even before their birth. The problem is, many believers and leaders are too lazy to find out what God has called them to do. They waste years trying to accomplish things that God never destined them for. Before a believer can effectively lead, it is imperative that he or she fully knows, without an iota of doubt, that he or she has been called of God to a particular task. That is the beginning point. It is the starting line.

"He Makes My Mouth like a Sharp Sword"

The leaders that God is making in this season of preparation will have mouths as sharp as a sword. Not mouths to criticize, grumble or murmur, but mouths for edification. The Word of God is spoken of as a sword in Ephesians 6:17. The Word is a sword that cuts under the flesh and the soul, down to the very intents of the heart (Hebrews 4:12).

"In the Shadow of His Hand Hath He Hid Me"

This speaks of the obscurity of the servant of the Lord during his/her time of preparation. During this time, the servant of the Lord is hidden from the eyes of the world and, sometimes, even from the eyes of the Church. Many of the leaders in the Bible experienced a "hidden" period. Moses, the great deliverer, was hidden forty years on the backside of the desert before he led his nation forth from Egypt. During this time, the Lord prepared a shepherd's heart in Moses, enabling him to lead the nation of Israel to freedom. The leaders that God is raising must learn to humbly abide under the shadow of the Almighty, in that secret place of preparation, without a spirit of impatience and distrust.

Jesus, the pattern Son, was under the shadow of the Almighty for thirty years before His unveiling at the river

Jordan. He was not released into His mighty ministry, to the nation nor ultimately to the world, until after His thirty "hidden" years. Moses, David, Elisha, Jesus, Paul and many more leaders experienced this period of overshadowing.

This principle still applies to the preparation of a leader today. Many leaders are going through this overshadowing right now. While some are chafing under it, others are taking advantage of it. What the Lord works into a leader during this period will be revealed at the time of the leader's release. Every servant of God should take advantage of this preparation time. It is an important period for the leader's future.

"He Also Made Me a Polished Shaft"

Here, the prophet brings forth a word, a picture of an arrow. He states that the shaft of the arrow must be polished before its use. The shaft is one of an arrow's most important components. If the shaft of the arrow is warped or misaligned in any way, the arrow will not hit its mark. A crooked shaft renders an arrow useless. The arrow's sharp head would be of little value if a malformed shaft made it miss the mark.

On the other hand, an arrow would also have little value if it reached its mark, but a dull head rendered it unable to stick. The arrow shaft and the arrow head are of equal importance. The shaft of the arrow can speak of the character of a servant of the Lord, while the head speaks of his ministry. Both the character and the ministry of a servant of God must be properly prepared.

The word "polish" means to clarify, to examine or to purge so as to brighten. Isaiah wrote that God had made him a polished shaft. The shaft must undergo the purging, sanding and polishing process to play its role in producing an arrow that will hit the mark.

During Isaiah's time, preparing an arrow was a tedious process. Acacia wood, a strong but very rough, crooked and knotted wood, had to be carefully straightened and sanded. First, all of the leaves were plucked from the chosen piece of wood. Next, the naked piece of wood was left in a frame, using tightly placed pegs that would slowly straighten it. The shaft was then anointed with oil to soften the wood before the final sanding. After sanding, the shaft was then ready to receive its tip.

All of these steps used in the preparation of a natural arrow speak of many spiritual truths in conjunction with the process of preparing a leader for this hour in the new move of God's Spirit. In a similar way, the Lord will take every leader through a stripping process before He uses him to hit the mark for which He was prepared. Every leader will experience character preparation (the straightening of the shaft) and ministerial preparation (sharpening of the head). This is a very painful and long process, at times. However, every leader can encourage himself in knowing that the more God plans to use an arrow, the more demanding will be their preparation.

"In His Quiver Hath He Hid Me"

The quiver experience is used for the "holding" purpose. A leader can enjoy a long wait until the chosen time that he or she goes forth. The "quiver experience" is very hard for most leaders, because they feel they have already taken the necessary steps of preparation to be sent forth. This is especially hard for those who have endured bitter experiences successfully. They have responded correctly to their calling, their word, their preparation, their hiding under God's hand, and their polishing. But now they ask, "Why the waiting period?"

This is a time when the leader learns patience. Because of this important lesson, the quiver is no less a place of preparation than the sanding block. The main importance in the quiver experience is not the external, but the internal. This is always the hardest test for any leader of the Lord. Each must realize that God has a perfect time when, as an arrow, he is shot forth to hit the mark that God has ordained for him.

> **But when the fullness of time was come, God sent forth his Son, made of a woman, made under the law.**
>
> **Galatians 4:4**

Paul stated here that the Lord Jesus was shot forth "in the fullness of time." Jesus came to earth in the perfect moment of history. This arrow had been waiting for at least four thousand years to be sent forth. But Jesus, who was the Lamb slain before the foundation of the world, waited patiently for the "fullness of time" to manifest in which He would be made known to the world.

David was destined to be a king of Israel. He was anointed when he was about seventeen years of age, but did not receive the throne until he was thirty. Such a great span or space of time. David had to wait in the quiver for thirteen years. Several times, David could have killed Saul to gain the throne by natural means, but the Lord gave him the grace to know that He would open the throne to David in His own way. David chose to wait for God's timing, and not man's.

Every leader has a special season set aside to "hide in the quiver." He or she will be revealed only at His appointed time. Temptation and pressure will come to every leader, from without and from within, urging him to go ahead of God's timing. God's leader must take great care to avoid tampering with the perfect timing of the Lord. There is no set age for the release of a leader. There is no set pattern for a leader to follow regarding release into ministry. The time and manner of release is different for every leader. This is why no leader should compare one's self to another. Each should wait patiently for the timing of the Lord, for He is the only perfect marksman.

CHAPTER 4

THE RECOGNITION OF CHARACTER

The U.S. Marine Corps recruiters say that they are "looking for a few good men." Not everyone qualifies for this highly disciplined and well-respected company of soldiers who usually lead forces into battle. Recruits must survive a series of grueling physical and mental tests before they become full-fledged Marines.

Jesus Christ is looking for a few good men to lead His Church, and to be models of Godly attitudes and ethics. This should be the mark of all mature Christians. He is extremely selective about who will guide His troops into spiritual battle, and who should care for and nurture His people.

The qualifications are extensive and essential to the spiritual health of a congregation. To compromise any standard is to risk defamation of character and morale within the Body, including an ineffective testimony in the world. Many of our churches are experiencing a lack of godliness and effectiveness, because of a failure to train and select men of integrity.

Who Qualifies to Be a Leader in this Hour?

During local, state and national election campaigns, voters are barraged by the claims of candidates who attempt to convince the electorate that they are the most qualified to be President, senator, legislator, governor, mayor, councilman or some other public official. Campaign rhetoric can be brutal. Unfortunately, the winner isn't always the most qualified person. The advantage often goes to the one with the best "media image." The biblical standards used for recognizing character maturity before leadership appointment are listed in the following:

> **THIS IS a true saying, If a man desires the office of a bishop, he desireth a good work.**
>
> **A bishop then must be blameless, the husband of one wife, vigilant, sober, of good behavior, given to hospitality, apt to teach;**
>
> **Not given to wine, no striker, not greedy of filthy lucre; but patient, not a brawler, not covetous;**
>
> **One that ruleth well his own house, having his children in subjection with all gravity;**
>
> **(For if a man know not how to rule his own house, how shall he take care of the church of God?)**
>
> **Not a novice, lest being lifted up with pride he fall into the condemnation of the devil.**

Moreover he must have a good report of them which are without; lest he fall into reproach and the snare of the devil.

Likewise *must* the deacons *be* grave, not double-tongued, not given to much wine, not greedy of filthy lucre;

Holding the mystery of the faith in a pure conscience.

I Timothy 3:1-9

For this cause left I thee in Crete, that thou shouldest set in order the things that are wanting, and ordain elders in every city, as I had appointed thee:

If any be blameless, the husband of one wife, having faithful children not accused of riot or unruly.

For a bishop must be blameless, as the steward of God; not self-willed, not soon angry, not given to wine, no striker; not given to filthy lucre;

But a lover of hospitality, a lover of good men, sober, just, holy, temperate;

Holding fast the faithful word as he hath been taught that he may be able by sound doctrine both to exhort and to convince the gainsayers.

Titus 1:5-9

I have highlighted these character qualities, and have grouped them into six categories. This will allow you, the reader, to better see them more clearly. They are as follows:

1. A good reputation.
2. Self-control
3. Godly values
4. A loving heart
5. A healthy home
6. A teachable mind

A Good Reputation

An old maxim states, "A chain is only as strong as its weakest link." This is quite true when seen in the light of the Church's character today. A leader may have great talent and extensive knowledge of the truths of the Bible, but if his life is as a "weak link," his reputation will suffer great damage and his ministry will be diminished, if not destroyed completely. This is why this first group of qualifications is vital to the Church today.

Blameless

> **A bishop then must be blameless, the husband of one wife, vigilant, sober, of good behavior, given to hospitality, apt to teach.**

And let these also first be proved; then let them use the office of a deacon, being *found* blameless.

I Timothy 3:2, 10

If any be blameless, the husband of one wife, having faithful children not accused of riot or unruly.

For a bishop must be blameless as the steward of God; not self-willed, not soon angry, not given to wine, no striker, not given to filthy lucre.

Titus 1:6, 7

These are all inclusive qualities relating to every area of our lives. It is important for the Body of Christ to live above reproach. When tested, they must be found "blameless" in the sight of the people they will be ministering to. Does this mean that a Christian has to be perfect to be a leader? Obviously not. No one is perfect. But the characteristic pattern of his life, must be in line with the biblical standards.

A Good Testimony Among Those Outside

Moreover he must have a good report of them which are without; lest he fall into reproach and the snare of the devil.

I Timothy 3:7

Those "outside" are non-Christians who observe the testimony of the Church. You cannot function properly in this hour, and witness in your community, if a cloud of disgrace hangs over your head because of questionable or clearly sinful activity. If your character is in question, it is not only detrimental to the Church, but it is also detrimental for the individual.

Of Good Behavior

> **A bishop then must be blameless, the husband of one wife, vigilant, sober, of good behavior, given to hospitality, apt to teach.**
>
> **I Timothy 3:2**

The word translated "good behavior" can also be translated "respectable" or "honorable." It comes from the Greek word for "orderly" or "well-arranged." A man who lives an orderly life is conducting himself in an honorable manner, thus earning the respect of those around him. To be effective, you must not be a Christian who runs from crisis to crisis because of your own disorganization. Your life must reflect consistency and order.

Self-control

An addict is a person who has lost control of his life. The controlling factor may be cocaine, alcohol, food, sex, TV, anger, money, power, work or an all-consuming hobby. In each case, the person is controlled instead of being in control. In contrast, God's leaders today must exhibit self- control.

But, what does it mean to be self-controlled? Paul's list of qualifications specifically mentions self-control and several other related items.

But a lover of hospitality, a lover of good men, sober, just, holy, temperate;

Titus 1:8

A leader must exhibit a disciplined life. He or she must demonstrate a growing Christ-likeness, and be in control of his or her passions and appetites. This self-control is not merely self-effort. It is cooperating with the indwelling Spirit to make wise choices and to live in dependence on Him. A self-controlled person chooses to live for God, instead of self. His life is in order. He is not in bondage to sinful impulses.

Not Given to Wine

Not given to wine, no striker, not greedy of filthy lucre; but patient, not a brawler, not covetous;

One that ruleth well his own house, having his children in subjection with all gravity;

(For if a man know not how to rule his own house, how shall he take care of the church of God?)

Not a novice, lest being lifted up with pride he fall into the condemnation of the devil.

Moreover he must have a good report of them which are without; lest he fall into reproach and the snare of the devil.

Likewise *must* the deacons *be* grave, not double-tongued, not given to much wine, not greedy of filthy lucre;

I Timothy 3:3-8

For a bishop must be blameless, as the steward of God; not self-willed, not soon angry, not given to wine, no striker, not given to filthy lucre;

Titus 1:7

The Greek word used in I Timothy 3:3 and Titus 1:7 refers to a habit of overdrinking. In classical and Hellenistic Greek times, the term had the meaning of being "tipsy" or "rowdy." The Greek word used in I Timothy 3:8 meant "to be attached to" or "addicted to" wine.

Paul warns against the overindulgence of wine – of being known as someone who gets drunk or spends much time drinking. Such a person will not be a worthy example, for he would fall into the danger of being controlled by wine, instead of by the Spirit (Eph. 5:18).

Not Quarrelsome

Not given to wine, no striker, not greedy of filthy lucre; but patient, not a brawler, not covetous.

I Timothy 3:3

For a leader to be successful and effective in the things of the Spirit of God, that individual must not be commonly given to argument, disputation, controversy, and rivalry. A mature person should be able to compromise on nonessential matters.

Not Self-willed

For a bishop must be blameless, as the steward of God; not self-willed, not soon angry, not given to wine, no striker, not given to filthy lucre.

Titus 1:7

A leader who is overbearing and inconsiderate is not qualified to lead God's people. Neither is someone who has consistently displayed an insensitive desire to have his way, regardless of facts, circumstances, and the needs or feelings of people.

Not Quick-tempered

For a bishop must be blameless as the steward of God; not self-willed, not soon angry, not given to wine, no striker, not given to filthy lucre.

Titus 1:7

A quick tempered leader destroys the work of God. He gets angry and belligerent very easily.

Not Double-tongued

Likewise *must* the deacons *be* grave, not double-tongued, not given to much wine, not greedy of filthy lucre;

I Timothy 3:8

God's leaders will be leaders whose word can be trusted. They will not be inconsistent or insincere in what they say. They cannot say one thing to one person, and something contradictory to another. Their "yes" must mean "yes," and their "no" must mean "no."

Godly Values

Would you be devastated if a thief stole your VCR and television? How would you react if your life savings vanished with an investment broker? Do you spend more time waxing your car than spending time with the Lord? Does your job consume all of your thoughts and energy? Do you take time to pray and read the Bible? What does your checkbook or your credit card statement say about your values? These are the kinds of questions that reveal what we treasure most in life.

Not Greedy for Money

> **Not given to wine, no striker, not greedy of filthy lucre; but patient, not a brawler, not covetous;**
>
> **One that ruleth well his own house, having his children in subjection with all gravity;**
>
> **(For if a man know not how to rule his own house, how shall he take care of the church of God?)**
>
> **Not a novice, lest being lifted up with pride he fall into the condemnation of the devil.**

Moreover he must have a good report of them which are without; lest he fall into reproach and the snare of the devil.

Likewise *must* the deacons *be* grave, not double-tongued, not given to much wine, not greedy of filthy lucre;

I Timothy 3:3-8

For a bishop must be blameless, as the steward of God; not self-willed, not soon angry, not given to wine, no striker, not given to filthy lucre.

Titus 1:7

The priorities of God's leaders must not be centered upon the accumulation of worldly wealth. Every leader must be a good illustration of one who, though he may be wealthy, places his greatest priority upon laying up treasure in heaven. No one should be able to accuse God's leaders of using his or her position for personal financial gain.

Not Covetous

Not given to wine, no striker, not greedy of filthy lucre; but patient, not a brawler, not covetous;

I Timothy 3:3

This quality is closely related to "not greedy for money." God's people, the Church, cannot be preoccupied with material wealth. The love of money can lead a believer away from the faith.

A Lover of What Is Good

But a lover of hospitality, a lover of good men, sober, just, holy, temperate;

Titus 1:8

In his commentary on Titus, William Hendricksen stated that "a lover of what is good" means "loving goodness, virtuous, ready to do what is beneficial to others." It refers to a person who desires to do good, not evil. In Galatians 6:10, the apostle Paul stated, "therefore, as we have opportunity, let us do good to all, especially to those who are of the household of faith." A "lover of what is good," then, means that such a person shows, by his or her actions, that he or she desires to reflect God's goodness in all that he or she does, and in all of his or her relationships. He or she has the best interests of others in mind.

His Children Are Obedient and Respectful

One that ruleth well his own house, having his children in subjection with all gravity;

I Timothy 3:4

If any be blameless, the husband of one wife, having faithful children not accused of riot or unruly.

Titus 1:6

This is a more specific statement of how God's leaders are supposed to manage their own houses. Our children are to show evidence that their father is a respected leader at home, and that he knows how to instruct and discipline them. No father has perfect children, so we shouldn't expect perfection. But, as Titus 1:6 states, the children should behave in such a manner that no one can accuse them of being wild and insubordinate.

Holy

> **But a lover of hospitality, a lover of good men, sober, just, holy, temperate;**
>
> **Titus 1:8**

God's leaders must develop an earnest desire to be pleasing to God. Their attitudes and actions must reflect devotedness – a devotion to God. They must place a high priority upon spiritual development in their lives, and their lives should reflect that their hearts are centered upon God and His Kingdom, not upon worldly things. This quality may seem somewhat difficult to attain but, with God nothing is impossible.

A Loving Heart

In I Corinthians 13, the apostle Paul, exhorted the supremacy that love should have as a characteristic of our lives. It is no wonder that Paul included several requirements that are indicative of a leadership candidate's love for others.

The following qualifications are various aspects of how God's leaders are to express love.

Gentle

Not given to wine, no striker, not greedy of filthy lucre; but patient, not a brawler, not covetous;

I Timothy 3:3

The exact meaning of this term is much broader than that which can be expressed with one word. The following terms approximate the meaning of the original Greek word: gracious, kind, forebearing, considerate, magnanimous and genial. A believer who is short-tempered, inconsiderate, rude, or cruel, would not be qualified for leadership.

Not Violent - (I Timothy 3:3) Literally, the Greek word means "not a striker." A leader of God's people cannot be one who displays a short temper, or resorts to intimidation in order to control others. Nor does he or she walk around with a "chip on his shoulder," looking for someone to knock it off. He or she cannot seek to settle his or her differences of opinion with violent words or actions. The fight is with the enemy, the devil, and not with our fellow brothers and sisters.

Hospitable - (I Timothy 3:2, Titus 1:8) This term literally means loving "strangers." In New Testament times, this quality referred to the action of befriending, and giving lodging to fellow believers who were traveling or fleeing persecution because of their faith in Christ. In a broader sense, to be hospitable refers to friendliness and a willingness to help others who need assistance, and this must be a characteristic of God's leaders.

A Healthy Home

Would you hire an auto mechanic who drives a sputtering, smoking pile of rusting junk? Or, would you ask a dental hygienist with decayed teeth to instruct you on how to keep your teeth in good condition? Would you want a person who has been in five auto accidents within the last year to give you some driving tips?

We expect the person with whom we entrust possessions and our lives to have some proven expertise, and to know what he is talking about. The same is true of God's leaders. They must practice what they preach and be good examples. A person's home life is the most revealing aspect of his character. They say, "charity begins at home." This is why Paul, in the lists he presents in I Timothy and in Titus, gives four qualifications that deal with the spiritual health of a believer's home.

He Is the Husband of One Wife - (I Timothy 3:2, 12; Titus 1:6) Good Bible scholars offer differing explanations of this requirement. Some say that a believer can be married only once during his lifetime. Others say that it means only that a believer must be married to one woman at a time. Another view is that a believer must be faithful to his wife, "a one-woman kind of man." At the very least, this qualification or characteristic requires that if a believer is married, he must be faithfully devoted to his wife. He must not be an adulterer, a man who keeps a mistress or a flirtatious person.

He Manages His House Well - (I Timothy 3: 4, 12) Paul made the observations that a man who cannot govern his own household can hardly be trusted to govern the Church. His children should be properly trained, and he must have a good relationship with his wife. This qualification may also include financial management. As the head of the family, a man must demonstrate the characteristics that will make him a fitting believer for a congregation.

Teachable Mind

Some people can be as stubborn as a mule. No matter how you reason with them, they refuse to listen. Once they make up their minds, they don't want to be confused with the facts. God's people should be able to discuss conflicting ideas and come to wise decisions. That is why Paul listed several characteristics of a qualified leader that reflect the ability to think objectively.

All of the qualities here are essential character traits for every believer in these last days.

Able to Teach - (I Timothy 3:2) This is a key qualification, with two shades of meaning. First, it may mean that God's leaders in this hour must be able to instruct others regarding biblical truths. But, the Greek word means to be "teachable." It means to teach in a skillful manner, able to teach, resulting from having been taught. It refers to a quality of life: humble, sensitive, desirous to know the will of God. Those who are apt to teach are also apt to learn. They learn more of the Word.

Temperate - (I Timothy 3:2) This word means more than just moderation in eating or drinking. It states that "a man who is temperate does not lose his physical, psychological and spiritual orientation. He remains stable and steadfast, and his thinking is clear." He is balanced in his living, not prone to destructive extremes.

Sober Minded - (I Timothy 3:2, Titus 1:8) The meaning of this word is very closely related to the previous term, temperate. God's leaders must be sensible in their thinking and actions. They cannot be someone who is prone to act upon impulse, or make rash and irrational decisions. They must be self-controlled and prudent in their actions. They must avoid quick decisions based upon inadequate information, and must generally exhibit sound judgment.

Just - (Titus 1:8) This is to be righteous, equitable and upright. This entails not only right-standing before God, but also doing what is right and just in one's dealings with other people. It is conduct that meets the approval of the Divine Judge. The just man is equitable in character, fair in decisions, correct in judgment, and upright and fair-minded. The just man can make mature decisions and proper judgments.

CHAPTER 5

THE REED NATURE VERSUS THE STONE NATURE

The apostle, Peter, is a picture of hope to all would-be leaders who have suffered from failure and disappointment. This century seems to be plagued with weak leadership in every area of life, from political to social and spiritual institutions. But the apostle Peter, is chosen as a model for weak leaders because he didn't remain a weak leader. He changed, to become a dynamic, strong leader of his generation.

The Spirit of Instability

We have leaders and would-be leaders who have great giftings, and yet have unstable character. God never rewards giftings. God rewards character and maturity. God's promotional strategy is not just on giftings. It is gifting mixed with character. The spirit of instability is a type of the reed nature.

> **Confidence in an unfaithful man in time of trouble is like a broken tooth, and a foot out of joint.**
>
> **Proverb 25:19**

Leaders who are unstable are easily moved by circumstances and are undependable. These individuals cannot be trusted with responsibilities, and are sometimes unable to discern the differences between right and wrong responsibilities. They may look good, have great personalities, charisma and even desire to serve God. But, the problem is they cannot transform desire into action. You don't put confidence in an unstable leader. They will disappoint and break your heart during time of battle.

What Is a Reed?

> **Now the rest of the acts of Jehoash which he did, and his might, and how he fought with Amaziah king of Judah, *are* they not written in the book of the chronicles of the kings of Judah?**
>
> **II Kings 14:15**
>
> **Now behold, thou trustest upon the staff of this bruised reed, *even* upon Egypt, on which if a man lean, it will go into his hand, and pierce it: so *is* Pharaoh king of Egypt unto all that trust on him.**
>
> **II Kings 18:21**
>
> **A bruised reed shall he not break, and the smoking flax shall he not quench: he shall bring forth judgment unto truth.**
>
> **Isaiah 42:3**

The Hebrew word for reed is *kaneh*, and this refers to a reed that grows in swamps and marshes. It is used in Scripture to symbolize weakness and fragility because of its hollowness. Later, in Greek, this came to mean "rod." Metaphorically, it meant rule or standard of excellence. Reeds were used to fence crops and hedges, and also as musical instruments, as well as for scales and ink pens.

Characteristics of the Reed Nature

The first characteristic of an individual with a reed nature is that they are impulsive. Herod was quick to come to the conclusion that Jesus was John the Baptist risen from the dead. The reason for the impulsive conclusion was the wrong interpretation of the fame of Jesus. That is always the nature of a reed leader. They are very impulsive.

> **And said unto his servants, This is John the Baptist; he is risen from the dead; and therefore mighty works do show forth themselves in him.**
>
> **Matthew 14:2**

Second, they are slow to understand the significance of spiritual things. Because of the instability of their nature, the reed kind of leader is slow to discern the significance of spiritual things. Most times this is damaging to their ability to govern, especially as a leader. Jesus in Scripture had to emphasize to the multitude the importance of hearing and understanding what you hear, because that is what helps to bring understanding to the things of God.

> **And he called the multitude, and said unto them, Hear, and understand:**

Not that which goeth into the mouth defileth a man; but that which cometh out of the mouth, this defileth a man.

Then came his disciples, and said unto him, Knowest thou that the Pharisees were offended, after they heard this saying?

But he answered and said, Every plant, which my heavenly Father hath not planted, shall be rooted up.

Let them alone: they be blind leaders of the blind. And if the blind lead the blind, both shall fall into the ditch.

Then answered Peter and said unto him, Declare unto us this parable.

And Jesus said, Are ye also yet without understanding?

Do not ye yet understand, that whatsoever entereth in at the mouth goeth into the belly, and is cast out into the draught?

But those things which proceed out of the mouth come forth from the heart; and they defile the man.

For out of the heart proceed evil thoughts, murders, adulteries, fornications, thefts, false witness, blasphemies:

These are the things which defile a man: but to eat with unwashen hands defileth not a man.

Matthew 15:10-20

Third, they become quickly overconfident after receiving spiritual enlightenment. This results in spiritual pride, which produces spiritual presumptuousness.

> **And Simon Peter answered and said, Thou art the Christ, the Son of the living God.**
>
> **And Jesus answered and said unto him, Blessed art thou, Simon Bar-jona: for flesh and blood hath not revealed it unto thee, but my Father which is in heaven.**
>
> **From that time forth began Jesus to show unto his disciples, how that he must go unto Jerusalem, and suffer many things of the elders and chief priests and scribes, and be killed, and be raised again the third day.**
>
> **Then Peter took him, and began to rebuke him, saying, be it far from thee, Lord: this shall not be unto thee.**
>
> **But he turned, and said unto Peter, Get thee behind me, Satan: thou art an offence unto me: for thou savourest not the things that be of God, but those that be of men.**
>
> **Matthew 16:16-17, 21-23**

Fourth, they misinterpret clear teachings.

> **Then Jesus answered and said, O faithless and perverse generation, how long shall I be with you? how long shall I suffer you? bring him hither to me.**
>
> **And Jesus rebuked the devil; and he departed out of him: and the child was cured from that very hour.**

Then came the disciples to Jesus apart, and said, Why could not we cast him out?

And Jesus said unto them, Because of your unbelief: for verily I say unto you, If ye have faith as a grain of mustard seed, ye shall say unto this mountain, Remove hence to yonder place; and it shall remove; and nothing shall be impossible unto you.

Howbeit this kind goeth not out but by prayer and fasting.

And while they abode in Galilee, Jesus said unto them, The Son of man shall be betrayed into the hands of men:

And they shall kill him, and the third day he shall be raised again. And they were exceeding sorry.

And when they were come to Capernaum, they that received tribute money came to Peter, and said, Doth not your master pay tribute?

Matthew 17:17-24

Fifth, they are carried away by carnal ambition.

Then answered Peter and said unto him, Behold, we have forsaken all, and followed thee; what shall we have therefore?

Matthew 19:27

And he cometh unto the disciples, and findeth them asleep, and saith unto Peter, What, could ye not watch with me one hour?

Matthew 26:40

Sixth, they are unable to discern the importance of key situations.

> **Then Simon Peter having a sword drew it, and smote the high priest's servant, and cut off his right ear. The servant's name was Malchus.**
>
> **John 18:10**

Another characteristic is that they respond emotionally to pressure.

> **AND JACOB called unto his sons, and said, gather yourselves together, that I may tell you that which shall befall you in the last days.**
>
> **Gather yourselves together, and hear, ye sons of Jacob; and hearken unto Israel your father.**
>
> **Reuben, thou art my firstborn, my might, and the beginning of my strength, the excellency of dignity, and the excellency of power:**
>
> **Unstable as water, thou shalt not excel; because thou wentest up to thy father's bed; then defiledst thou it: he went up to my couch.**
>
> **Genesis 49:1-4**

Finally, they are very unstable.

The Stone Nature

> **And he brought him to Jesus. And when Jesus beheld him, he said, Thou art Simon the son of Jona:**

thou shalt be called Cephas, which is by interpretation, A stone.

John 1:42

Ye also, as lively stones, are built up a spiritual house, an holy priesthood, to offer up spiritual sacrifices, acceptable to God by Jesus Christ.

I Peter 2:5

And he took his staff in his hand, and chose him five smooth stones out of the brook, and put them in a shepherd's bag which he had, even in a scrip; and his sling was in his hand: and he drew near to the Philistine.

I Samuel 17:40

The Scripture describes us as lively stones that are built up. That is the stone nature in a leader. Peter, after his transformation, possessed this nature. He was called a "stone." David, in fighting against Goliath, used five smooth stones and was victorious. Even though there were physical stones in his hands, David's nature in the face of adversity, crisis and the taunting of Goliath was a picture of a leader who is stable, fixed and focused. He had a stone nature.

The stone nature is a nature of stability. Christians who possess this nature are individuals who are stable as leaders, know where they fit and function there faithfully. They follow guidelines and accept their limitations. Usually, the leaders with the stone nature are never carried away by fame and popularity. They consistently supply quiet strength and long-lasting stability, with visible joy and contentment in their places of leadership.

How to Be Changed from the Reed Nature to the Stone Nature

1) In order to change from the reed nature to the stone nature, we must be willing to accept the conviction that God has placed in us for His pleasure and purpose.

2) Second, we must be willing to destroy old spiritual roots by committing ourselves to the new God-ordained place He has chosen for us.

Moreover I will appoint a place for my people Israel, and will plant them, that they may dwell in a place of their own, and move no more; neither shall the children of wickedness afflict them any more, as beforetime,

II Samuel 7:10

The righteous shall flourish like the palm tree: he shall grow like a cedar in Lebanon.

Those that be planted in the house of the LORD shall flourish in the courts of our God.

They shall still bring forth fruit in old age; they shall be fat and flourishing;

Psalm 92:12-14

3) Third, we must respond to God's planting. We must allow time for our roots to bear fruit. The righteous bears fruit and his root is firm.

The wicked desireth the net of evil men: but the root of the righteous yieldeth fruit.

Proverbs 12:12

4) Fourth, we must be prepared to oppose anything that would cause us to leave the place of our planting. The place of our planting is the place of your harvest and you must not allow anything to uproot you.

If the spirit of the ruler rise up against thee, leave not thy place; for yielding pacifieth great offences.

Ecclesiastes 10:4

5) Finally, we must be willing to commit ourselves, our resources, our talents, and our energy to serve unselfishly and sacrificially. It is through serving that promotion comes. However, you must be able to know your place in the body, because God has set us in His body as He pleases. When we understand this, we will not think more highly of ourselves than we ought to think.

But now hath God set the members every one of them in the body, as it hath pleased him.

I Corinthians 12:18

For I say, through the grace given unto me, to every man that is among you, not to think of himself more highly than he ought to think; but to think soberly, according as God hath dealt to every man the measure of faith.

Romans 12:3

CHAPTER 6

THE PRINCIPLE OF PROMOTION

It is imperative that those aspiring to leadership, and those in leadership positions in the Body of Christ, understand God's principle of promotion and His process. Many times, leadership looks in the wrong places and at the wrong people for promotion. We consider those who faithfully clean the pews, the restrooms of the church, or cut the church's lawn as the most suitable candidates for promotion. While it is proper for the ministry of helps in a local fellowship to handle these responsibilities, those in leadership must realize that these are not the prerequisites for God's promotion. Man may promote you because you have worked very hard in his ministry but the question is, has God promoted you?

> **For not from the east nor from the west nor from the south come promotion and lifting up.**
>
> **But God is the judge. He puts down one and lifts up another.**
>
> **Psalm 75:6-7 AMP**

The Bible explicitly tells us who is the Source of promotion. It does not come from the east, the west, the south or the north. Nor does it emanate from man, father, mother, brother or any relative. Promotion comes from God. This is what God does; He puts down one and raises up another. There are many leaders in positions today that have been illegally promoted because of their affiliation to the promoter. We see parents in ministry who, as a result of their own desires, place their children in ministry positions of authority. Without asking God of His desires, their children are illegally promoted to positions within a church or ministry.

Then there is the group that is illegally promoted because they give large amounts of money to a church or ministry. God only installs leaders. The Scripture says that God puts down one and then lifts up another. That means that the route to every promotion is demotion. The more I determine to walk as a servant, the more I become a candidate for promotion. The way up is always down. That is the process. Men who have been promoted and elevated from a servanthood position can be easily identified. Their will and desire will be to please God, their promoter. When man promotes you, man can dethrone you. However when God promotes you, no man can dethrone you whether they like you or not. It is a simple principle. You will seek to please whoever promotes you. Therefore, if man promotes you, daily you will seek to please that man in order to keep your position. On the other hand, when God promotes you, daily you will seek to please Him in order to keep His anointing. Now, whose promotion do you want? Man's or God's?

Child of God, this is the hour that God is dethroning illegally promoted men and women in leadership positions, whether big or small. There is nothing wrong with parents in ministry desiring their children to be part of the work that God has given them. I believe that is the desire of every parent but we must not force them into ministry. We must allow God to have His way in their lives. They, like other leaders, must go through the "factory of God." They must be properly manufactured and marketed by God.

Eli and His Sons

> **Now the sons of Eli were sons of Belial; they knew not the Lord.**
>
> **And the priests' custom with the people was, that, when any man offered sacrifice, the priest's servant came, while the flesh was in seething, with a fleshhook of three teeth in his hand;**
>
> **And he struck it, into the pan, or kettle or caldron, or pot; all that the fleshhook brought up the priest took for himself. So they did in Shiloh, unto all the Israelites that came thither.**
>
> **Also before they burnt the fat, the priest's servant came, and said to the man that sacrificed, Give flesh to roast for the priest; for he will not have sodden flesh of thee, but raw.**
>
> **And if any man said unto him, Let them not fail to burn the fat presently, and then take as much as thy soul desireth; then he would answer him, Nay; but thou shalt give it me now: and if not, I will take it by force.**

> **Wherefore the sin of the young men was very great before the Lord: for men abhorred the offering of the Lord.**
>
> **I Samuel 2:12-17**

The sacreligious sons of Eli were a good example of men who were promoted because of their affiliation to the promoter. The Aaronic priesthood was represented by Eli's two sons, Hophni and Phinehas. Hophni means "he that covers my fist" or a "fighter," and Phinehas means "a bold countenance" or "brazen mouth." The Bible says, that when the children of Israel would come to Shiloh to offer up sacrifices to the Lord, Hophni and Phinehas would not only take more than the priest's share of their sacrifices, they were taking the fat, which was designated as the Lord's portion in Leviticus 1-7. The fat was to be burnt on the altar of God. When the people questioned whether the Lord received His portion, these priestly sons would take the offerings by force from the people. The result was that the people of God abhorred the offering of the Lord. They despised the atonement because of the way Eli's sons behaved. Their sins were very great before the Lord.

Men who are illegally promoted will take the "fat on the offerings," which is God's portion. They will heap up praise, glory and honor to themselves because they have not been properly manufactured in God's factory. They will have no fear of God or a desire to please Him, but they will always seek glory for themselves. They will make themselves "fat" at the expense of others.

Immoral Leaders

Now Eli was very old, and heard all that his sons did unto all Israel; and how they lay with the women that assembled at the door of the tabernacle of the congregation.

I Samuel 2:22

The sons of Eli also engaged in acts of immorality with the women who assembled at the tabernacle. Though the sons of Eli wore linen ephods and priestly robes – symbolic of righteousness, purity and holiness – their lives were not indicative of such. Again, this is characteristic of a leader who has not gone through God's factory. Don't you know that a position diligently earned is easier to keep than a position acquired because of skill or relationship with the leader?

Loose Promoters

And he said unto them, Why do ye such things? For I hear of your evil dealings by all this people.

Nay, my sons; for it is no good report that I hear: ye make the Lord's people to transgress.

If one man sin against another, the judge shall judge him: but if a man sin against the Lord, who shall entreat for him?

Notwithstanding, they hearkened not unto the voice of their father, because the Lord would slay them.

I Samuel 2:23-25

And the Lord said to Samuel, Behold, I will do a thing in Israel, at which both the ears of every one that heareth it shall tingle.

In that day I will perform against Eli all things which I have spoken concerning his house: when I begin, I will also make an end.

For I have told him that I will judge his house forever for the iniquity which he knoweth; because his sons made themselves vile, and he restrained them not.

And therefore I have sworn unto the house of Eli, that the iniquity of Eli's house shall not be purged with sacrifice nor offering forever.

I Samuel 3:11-14

Eli failed to restrain or discipline his sons properly. Although he knew of their immoral acts, he mildly reproved them. They should have been removed from the priesthood immediately when they failed to meet the qualifications. But, God would not touch them because they were under the covering of their father. As time went by, Eli still would not discipline his sons. Finally, God intervened and judged Eli and his two sons. In the matters of God's people there will be divine discipline, in the absence of human discipline. The Bible referred to Eli's sons, though priests of God's altar, as sons of Belial (I Samuel 2:12). They were no longer of the

Lord. Belial means "lawless, recklessness, worthless." Therefore, Hophni and Phinehas were sons of lawlessness and sons of recklessness. They were true to their interpreted names, "church saints and house devils." God's leaders must note that the one you promote within your ministry or church, whether a relative, friend or a congregational member, will either weaken and destroy, or strengthen and build up your ministry.

This was the problem with Eli (which means "the offering, the lifting up or going up"). He allowed his children to function in the priesthood, fully aware of their wicked behavior, then refused to discipline them. Because of this, his ministry was destroyed and his office was fulfilled by another person who was promoted by God.

The Promotional Parable

> **And all the men of Shechem gathered together, and all the house of Millo, and went, and made Abimelech king, by the plain of the pillar that was in Shechem.**
>
> **And when they told it to Jotham, he went and stood in the top of mount Gerizim, and lifted up his voice, and cried, and said unto them, Hearken unto me, ye men of Shechem, that God may hearken unto you.**
>
> **The trees went forth on a time to anoint a king over them; and they said unto the olive tree, Reign thou over us.**

But the olive tree said unto them, Should I leave my fatness, wherewith by me they honor God and man, and go to be promoted over the trees?

And the trees said unto them, Should I forsake my sweetness, and my good fruit, and go to be promoted over the trees?

Then said the trees unto the vine, Come thou, and reign over us.

And the vine said unto them, Should I leave my wine, which cheereth God and man, and go to be promoted over the trees? Then said all the trees unto the bramble, Come thou, and reign over us.

And the bramble said unto the trees, If in truth ye anoint me king over you, then come and put your trust in my shadow: and if not, let fire come out of the bramble, and devour cedars of Lebanon.

Now therefore, if ye have done truly and sincerely, in that ye have made Abimelech king, and if ye have dealt well with Jerubbabel and his house, and have done unto him according to the deserving of his hands;

For my father fought for you, and adventured his life far, and delivered you out of the hand of Midian:

And ye are risen up against my father's house this day, and have slain his sons, threescore and ten persons upon one stone, and have made Abimelech, the son of his maidservant, king over the men of Shechem, because he is your brother;

If you then have dealt truly and sincerely with Jerubbabel and with his house day, then rejoice ye in Abimelech, and let him also rejoice in you:

But if not, let fire come out from Abimelech, and devour the men of Shechem, and the house of Millo; and let fire come out from the men of Shechem, and from the house of Millo, and devour Abimelech.

And Jotham ran away, and fled and went to Beer, and dwelt there, for fear of Abimelech his brother.

When Abimelech had reigned three years over Israel,

Then God sent an evil spirit between Abimelech and the men of Shechem; and the men of Shechem dealt treacherously with Abimelech:

That the cruelty done to the threescore and ten sons of Jerubbabel might come, and their blood be laid upon Abimelech their brother, which slew them; and upon the men of Shechem, which aided him in the killing of his brethren.

And the men of Shechem set liers in wait for him in the top of the mountains and they robbed all that came along that way by them: and it was told Abimelech.

Then went Abimelech to Thebez, and encamped against Thebez, and took it.

But there was a strong tower within the city, and thither fled all the men and women, and all they of the city, and shut it to them, and gat them up to the top of the tower.

And Abimelech came unto the tower, and fought against it, and went hard unto the door of the tower to burn it with fire.

And a certain woman cast a piece of a millstone upon Abimelech's head, and all to brake his skull.

Then he called hastily unto the young man his armor bearer, and said unto him, Draw thy sword, and slay me, that men say not of me, A woman slew him. And his young man thrust him through and he died.

And when the men of Israel saw that Abimelech was dead, they departed every man unto his place.

Thus God rendered the wickedness of Abimelech, which he did unto his father, in slaying his seventy brethren:

And all the evil of the men of Shechem did God render upon their heads: and upon them came the curse of Jotham the son of Jerubbabel.

Judges 9:6-24, 50-57

This parable was born out of political turmoil and gives us a more in-depth understanding of God's principle of promotion. For a short time, the men of Shechem accepted Abimelech as their king. He was the son of Jerubbabel (Gideon) by his Shechemite concubine. Abimelech won the family fight among Gideon's seventy sons for rulership over the tribe of Manasseh. The Shechemites, who were mostly Canaanites, gladly conceded to Abimelech, because he had more blood ties to them than did the other sons of Gideon.

With the help of the Shechemites, Abimelech went to his father's house at Ophrah and murdered his seventy half-brothers with a single stone. Only Jotham, the youngest, escaped his hand. From the top of Mount Gerizim, Jotham quoted this beautiful parable of promotion.

Jotham's parable describes how all but one tree understood the position God had given them and were content to stay there. A believer who is truly promoted by God will be satisfied and content with what God has called him or her to be. Illegally promoted leaders never become satisfied and content. They always want more power. But God, in this hour, is raising up men and women who will be content with their leadership positions.

The Bramble Bush

The olive tree, the fig tree and the grapevine accepted their position in nature.

> **But the olive tree said unto them, Should I leave my fatness, wherewith by me they honor God and man, and go to be promoted over the trees?**
>
> **But the fig tree said unto them, Should I forsake my sweetness, and my good fruit, and go to be promoted over the trees?**
>
> **And the vine said unto them, Should I leave my wine, which cheereth God and man, and go to be promoted over the trees?**
>
> **And the bramble said unto the trees, if in truth ye anoint me king over you, then come and put your**

trust in my shadow: and if not, let fire come out of the bramble, and devour the cedars of Lebanon.

Judges 9:9, 11, 13, 15

The bramble bush, however, desired to go beyond the realm that God ordained for it. It wanted to be promoted over all the other trees and to upset the natural order of all things around it. There is an order set up for promotion. It is a spiritual order and it comes from God. God's order of promotion is different from man's order.

Judges 9:15 makes an interesting contrast of the bramble bush and the cedars of Lebanon. The bramble bush cannot in any way be compared to the ancient majestic cedars of Lebanon, neither can the bramble bush overshadow or replace them.

In order for the Body of Christ to be fully processed by God and to lead the people, they must adopt the attitude portrayed by the olive tree, the fig tree and the vine. These trees accepted their present and future status. The leaders God is raising up will accept the place in ministry God has given to them, and will stay within their boundaries until God promotes them again.

CHAPTER 7

BLIND LEADERS VERSUS SIGHTED LEADERS

God is raising up men and women with vision. For many years, blind leaders have been directing God's people. They have mounted God's holy pulpits declaring the Word of the Lord, yet they lack vision. How can the blind effectively lead? In His making process, God is raising up men and women who have both short-term and long-term vision in the spiritual realm. They can see, hear, receive and articulate God's messages for His people.

Blind leaders not only fail to properly discern the things of God in the spiritual realm, but also those in the physical realm. They are dull of hearing and cannot distinguish the voice of God, because their hearts are covered with a veil of darkness.

The Blind Leaders

> **And the child Samuel ministered unto the Lord before Eli. And the word of the Lord was precious in those days; there was no open vision.**

And it came to pass at that time, when Eli was laid down in his place, and his eyes began to wax dim, that he could not see;

And ere the lamp of God went out in the temple of the Lord, where the ark of God was, and Samuel was laid down to sleep;

That the Lord called Samuel: and he answered, Here am I.

And he ran unto Eli, and said, Here am I; for thou calledst me. And he said, I called not; lie down again. And he went and lay down.

And the Lord called yet again, Samuel. And Samuel arose and went to Eli, and said, Here am I; for thou didst call me. And he answered, I called not, my son; lie down again.

Now Samuel did not yet know the Lord, neither was the word of the Lord yet revealed unto him.

And the Lord called Samuel again the third time. And he arose and went to Eli, and said, Here am I; for thou didst call me. And Eli perceived that the Lord had called the child.

Therefore Eli said unto Samuel, Go, lie down: and it shall be, if he call thee, that thou shalt say, Speak, Lord; for they servant heareth. So Samuel went and lay down in his place.

And the Lord came, and stood, and called as at other times, Samuel, Samuel. Then Samuel answered, Speak; for thy servant heareth.

And the Lord said to Samuel, Behold, I will do a thing in Israel, at which both the ears of every one that heareth it shall tingle.

I Samuel 3:1-11

The above scripture describes the difference between the spiritually blind and the sighted, and beautifully portrays the making process of a God-promoted leader. Eli was a judge in Israel at that time, which meant he functioned as king, prophet, pastor, apostle, teacher and evangelist of his day. He was all in all. Men and women came from far and near to receive the Word of the Lord from Eli, to offer sacrifices, to get stirred up, and to be ministered to. Eli and his lawless sons ministered to the Lord at Shiloh, the spiritual center of Israel.

When a leader becomes blind to the "present" things of God, they cannot see, hear nor understand the "new things" of God. They hold onto the old things. They embrace the old and operate in what worked before their eyes began to wax dim. Their spiritual perception becomes dull, especially concerning hearing the voice and understanding the leading of God.

The Word of God shows us how during this time, Eli's eyes began to wax dim. He could no longer see, and the lamp of the Lord in the temple had gone out. This is very significant. It is important that the Body of Christ fully understand what is happening here. The eyes are the gate to your hearts. The eyes are the source of your vision. Eli's understanding and the vision God had placed upon his life including the anointing, had begun to wax dim. He could no longer comprehend the things of God. This is a dangerous place to find ourselves. We have leaders who are functioning like this today. Their eyes are growing increasingly dim. This group of individuals has led many Christians astray, and they are still leading many into ditches of ignorance, tradition, failure and defeat.

Temple of the Lord

When the eyes of a leader's understanding begin to wax dim, the lamp of his temple will gradually begin to dim. When this happens, the Word of the Lord will become precious, scarce, rare and infrequent in our church, ministry and land.

> **And what agreement hath the temple of God with idols? For ye are the temple of the living God; as God hath said I will dwell in them, and walk in them; and I will be their God, and they shall be my people.**
>
> **II Corinthians 6:16**

The Bible calls you and I the "temple of the living God." The physical church building that we attend every Sunday is not the temple. It is a place where we gather to fellowship with one another. But, the *real* temple is you and I. We are the temple of the Lord. Our temple must be kept clean. Our temple must remain "lit" with the glory of the Lord. We cannot afford to allow the lamp of our temple to grow dim. A leader cannot see and understand the things of God when his lamp is dim. Such individuals will begin to fellowship and walk in darkness because they lack understanding, direction and clarity in the things of God.

The Lamp of Our Temple

Temple lamps need oil and fire to produce light. When the oil which is a type of the anointing dries out, the lamp is extinguished. We must continually be filled to the brim with the anointing or our lamps will go out. When the temple is in darkness, spiritual eyesight and hearing begin to grow dull, and eventually stop functioning.

Because Eli neglected to discipline his incorrigible sons Hophni and Phinehas, he suffered great consequences. The ultimate result was that the oil in Eli's lamp dried up, his light went out, and God passed the baton.

This is illustrated in I Samuel, chapters 1 and 2. At one time Eli had an open connection with God. As a leader and priest, Eli communicated with God on a regular basis. When Hannah desired to bare a child for Elkanah, she came to Eli who went to the Lord on her behalf. Eli must have been walking upright and communicating regularly with God. Not only were the gates of communication open, Eli was witnessing answered prayers during this time. This is further validated by Eli's confidence in his ability to be a great spokesman for God in Shiloh, when he confronted the distressed Hannah after her prayer.

Eli answered, "Go in peace, and may the God of Israel grant you what you have asked of him." I Samuel 1:17 (NIV)

As the story continues, God answers the prayers of Hannah and gives her a son named Samuel which means "asked of God." In the meantime, Eli slowly began losing the favor of God. Why? Because he was ignoring the sinful lives that his sons were living before the Lord. The New American Standard Bible says that Eli's sons were worthless men and they did not know the Lord (vs. 12). The behavior of his sons, along with his own ignorance, was causing Eli's oil to dry up.

Many leaders today are witnessing their anointing gradually drying up because they are permitting all types of sin that is not pleasing to God. Some leaders are ignoring the drastic mistakes that their relatives, staff members, friends and ministers are making before the Lord, thus causing their oil to run dry. The responsibility of God's leaders is great, but it must be handled as God handles His, with no preferential differences. God is no respecter of persons, yet it is this very thing that is causing the eyes of our leaders to "wax dim." As the eyes of our leaders wax dim, the Word of the Lord becomes "scarce, infrequent and precious."

Clogged Pipes

Now Eli was very old, and he heard all that his sons were doing to all Israel, and how they lay with the women who served at the doorway of the tent of the meeting.

And he said to them, "Why do you do such things, the evil things that I hear from all these people?

No, my sons; for the report is not good which I hear the Lord's people circulating."

I Samuel 2:22-24 NASB

The Scripture pinpoints the position that Eli, as a leader, found himself in. We see Eli receiving "vital" information from the wrong source. Eli is now hearing from people and not from the Lord. Somewhere along the line, Eli's communicative pipeline to God became clogged. Surely, if God was not pleased with Eli's son's behavior, He would attempt to contact the leader. Eli was their natural father, but because Eli's pipes were clogged, he could no longer hear from God. Eli confronted his sons with data which he gathered from news that was circulating among the Lord's people.

Although the circulating data concerning his sons was accurate, this was a very dangerous position for a leader of God's people to be in. We have this situation existing in God's Church today. Many times, God's leaders allow their pipes (that connect to Him) to become clogged and have to rely on "circulating" data among the people. This places the leaders in a very susceptible position because they are open for the truth along with lies, rumors, assumptions, etc. It is paramount that our pipes remain free from debris. The leaders that God is making will cherish their pipeline and do everything possible to make sure that it is unclogged.

Because God knew Eli's pipes were clogged, He began preparation for a new leader to take the leadership position (in other words, the exchanging of the baton). The favor of God began to be evident in the life of Samuel.

> **Now the boy Samuel grew and was in favor both with the Lord and with men.**
>
> **I Samuel 2:26 AMP**

When our communication pipeline to God remains clogged, the Word of the Lord cannot reach us. This could prove to be very detrimental, especially to God's leaders who cannot afford to allow their pipes to rust. They run the risk of affecting entire nations and acquiring an inability to lead effectively.

The Bible describes Eli's clogged pipe as, "his eyes began to wax dim." What a portrait! Eli, a leader and priest, could no longer "see." How many of us desire leaders that cannot "see?" None. As a result, Eli's inability to "see" caused the Word of the Lord to be rare in those days and "visions were infrequent." I Samuel 3:1 (AMP). In other words, Eli's clogged pipes affected the entire nation. These types of leaders are misleading "nations" of God's people.

The Next Best Thing

Because God realized the state that Eli was in, He did not give up trying to communicate with him. While God was preparing Samuel, He sent a prophet to clear things up for Eli.

> **And there came a man of God unto Eli, and said unto him, Thus saith the LORD, Did I plainly**

appear unto the house of thy father, when they were in Egypt in Pharoah's house?

And did I choose him out of all the tribes of Israel to be my priest, to offer upon mine altar, to burn incense, to wear an ephod before me? and did I give unto the house of thy father all the offerings made by fire of the children of Israel?

Wherefore kick ye at my sacrifice and at mine offering, which I have commanded in my habitation; and honourest thy sons above me, to make yourselves fat with the chiefest of all the offerings of Israel my people?

Wherefore the LORD GOD of Israel saith, I said indeed that thy house, and the house of thy father, should walk before me for ever: but now the LORD saith, Be it far from me; for them that honour me I will honour, and they that despise me shall be lightly esteemed.

Behold, the days come, that I will cut off thine arm, and the arm of thy father's house, that there shall not be an old man in thine house.

And thou shalt see an enemy in my habitation, in all the wealth which God shall give Israel: and there shall not be an old man in thine house for ever.

And the man of thine, whom I shall not cut off from mine altar, shall be to consume thine eyes, and to grieve thine heart: and all the increase of thine house shall die in the flower of their age.

And this shall be a sign unto thee, that shall come upon thy two sons, on Hophni and Phinehas; in one day they shall die both of them.

And I will raise me up a faithful priest, that shall do according to that which is in mine heart and in my mind: and I will build him a sure house; and he shall walk before mine anointed for ever.

And it shall come to pass, that every one that is left in thine house shall come and crouch to him for a piece of silver and a morsel of bread, and shall say, Put me, I pray thee, into one of the priests' offices, that I may eat a piece of bread.

I Samuel 2:27-36

God has many ways of establishing his point. If we allow our pipes to clog, God will always use the next best thing to reach us. When God finally reaches us, the news may not always be pleasant as in the case of Eli.

Confidence Depleted

Eli once possessed great confidence in his relationship with God. This confidence resulted in great leadership ability in Eli. As Eli's eyes began to wax dim, his inability to pinpoint the moves of God grew stronger. He lost confidence in his ability to pinpoint what God was trying to communicate. This resulted in improper training for his protege, Samuel. Eli's oil so dried up, Samuel approached Eli three times before he even realized that God was at work.

The Lord called Samuel a third time, and Samuel got up and went to Eli and said, "Here I am; you called me."

Then Eli realized that the Lord was calling the boy.

So Eli told Samuel, "Go and lie down, and if he calls you, say, "Speak, Lord, for your servant is listening."

"What was it he said to you?" Eli asked.

I Samuel 3:8-9a, 17a NIV

This is a sad state for a leader to be in. Here we see a leader who is unable to realize God's call upon the life of one of His servants. After God called Samuel three times, the Bible says that Eli "realized" the Lord was calling. This could actually have been done with human reasoning in the flesh. This type of realization can take place without the power of God. Eli took the two previous occurrences of Samuel's beckoning to mean, "Oh yeah, Samuel, I realize God is calling you." Spare us all from this type of leadership! Then Eli spoke and exhibited his level of confidence. He said, "Go and lie down, and *if* he calls you . . ." Confident people, especially leaders, do not use the word, "if." Confident people say "when."

Eli's priestly career was now in a state of stagnation. His confidence was depleted. We see a leader who advises his protege saying, "Well, if this happens, do this!" Interestingly, the next day, Eli asked Samuel, "What was it He said to you?" Poor Eli. It was time to pass the baton now. His time had obviously expired.

In these last days of the Church, we will see leaders whose confidence reigns supreme in their God and in their relationship with Him. They will treasure their pipeline to Him. They will continuously run "spiritual drano" through their pipes to keep it free from debris. Their confidence will attract many people to follow them and get direction from the Lord anew! These are the men and women that God is making in His factory. God has been manufacturing them. This present move of God will demonstrate the emergence of these leaders. When you see them, you will realize that they have been with God. The love of God and the desire to please God will burn like fire in their bones. They will not be promoted by men. Their making, their advertisement and their marketing will be done by God Himself.

Sighted Leaders

The sighted leader is one who makes sure there is always fresh oil in his lamp. He makes certain that it is always filled to the brim with the anointing of the Holy Spirit. He constantly checks his spiritual gauge to ensure that he is always filled up. He can see, hear and understand. His eyes do not wax dim because the lamp of his temple is continuously filled with oil; the temple is always lit. He will not stumble, because he can see. He can discern between good and evil. His spiritual antenna is so keen, he can pick up all of God's "radar."

> **And ere the lamp of God went out in the temple of the Lord, where the ark of God was, and Samuel was laid down to sleep.**
>
> **I Samuel 3:3**

Samuel was an example of this kind of leader. He was a sighted leader. He could see, hear and understand the things of God. The Scripture lets us know that Samuel laid down to sleep. He slept close to the ark of God, which represented the presence and glory of God. The ark of God was in the temple. We are the temple of God, so we have the ark of God – the presence and the glory of God in us. Samuel had the presence of God in him, even though the lamp in Eli's temple was gradually fading and his eyes increasingly darkened to where he could not see. In the midst of corrupt, insincere, undedicated and uncommitted leaders, God is raising up leaders who will cherish and abide in the presence and the glory of God daily.

> **That the Lord called Samuel: and he answered, Here am I.**
>
> **I Samuel 3:4**

When the Lord called Samuel, he answered even though he did not know who was calling him. The key word here is that he answered. Many times, we ask too many questions. All we need to do is to answer when He calls. We may not know where we are being sent. We may not have the finances to survive. We may not have all of the Bible school education and knowledge but because HE called, we will answer.

When we learn to answer the call of God without hesitation and resistance, God will show us the "new thing." He will unfold and complete the riddle of our lives. He will show us the direction to take.

Because Samuel did not fully understand his call, he went to Eli. Samuel thought Eli would understand, but he did not. His lamp had already gone out and his eyes had waxed dim. Child of God, you have to be very careful who you approach in confirming your call. You may find yourself going to the wrong person, and he or she can hinder God's direction for your life. A man or woman who cannot discern and understand the voice of God, cannot accurately confirm your call.

Many times, leaders who have people in essential positions in their churches and ministries, find it difficult to release their members when God begins to call them. They become concerned over who will replace these called ones. As a result, they resort to using every strategy to discourage them from fulfilling their callings. Some might say, "You are in too much of a hurry." The Word tells us that being in haste or in a hurry is wrong. However, dragging your feet concerning the call of God is also wrong. The best place to be is side by side with God, flowing in perfect timing in your walk with the Lord.

I strongly believe in this move of God's Spirit that leaders of churches and ministries will sense the call of God upon the lives of their members, and will hasten to train and release them to their own ministries. Like a parent, they will set them up in their ministries. They will help them find a place to fellowship and participate in the opening of their ministries. The Body of Christ, like never before, will see masters releasing their servants unselfishly.

The Second Call

And the Lord called yet again, Samuel. And Samuel arose and went to Eli, and said,

Here am I; for thou didst call me. And he answered, I called not, my son; lie down again.

I Samuel 3:6

The Lord again called and Samuel answered. Because he still did not understand his calling, he could not *respond* to the call. He went to Eli, thinking he was the one calling him. But Eli said, "I did not call you, go back to bed." One might expect that as a leader Eli would have realized the first time God called Samuel. Eli was Samuel's leader and mentor. It is dangerous to be under a leader or mentor who does not flow in the realm of the Spirit. Eli should have known immediately, when Samuel came saying that someone was calling his name.

Because the lamp in Eli's temple was already out, and his eyes of understanding were waxing dim, he could not discern the voice of God from the voice of man. There are many aspiring leaders today that are being led by leaders with the same spirit of Eli. God will not tolerate ill perception in this hour. If you are under such a leader, get from under that umbrella and seek the Lord to lead you elsewhere.

The Third Call

And the Lord called Samuel again the third time. And he arose and went to Eli, and said, Here am I;

> **for thou didst call me. And Eli perceived that the Lord had called the child.**
>
> **I Samuel 3:8**

It wasn't until the third time that Eli finally *perceived* that God was indeed calling Samuel. I would not follow a leader who is unable to discern the moves of God, nor able to hear the voice of God. I want a leader who is highly sensitive, sharp and can immediately pinpoint the move and leading of God.

Faith in Operation

Samuel learned the principle which I believe every aspiring leader and believer must know and walk in. That is, the principle of faith.

> **Therefore Eli said unto Samuel, Go, lie down: and it shall be, if he call thee, that thou shalt say, Speak, Lord; for thy servant heareth. So Samuel went and lay down in his place.**
>
> **I Samuel 3:9**

Eli told Samuel, "When you hear the voice again, you say to the voice, 'Speak, Lord, for thy servant heareth.'" This is an important principle that must be learned, especially in launching out. Samuel did not see, smell, taste or touch God. He did not even know that it was God calling him. He learned that all he needed to do was launch out in faith, and God would meet him at the point of launching out. Launching out and risking everything is the point when God begins to respond. We may not know or understand the entire plan and purpose for our lives, but as we begin to launch out in faith, believing that the steps of the righteous are ordered by the Lord, God will begin to direct our paths.

That is exactly what Eli told Samuel to do. "Launch out in faith." By faith, say to that voice, "Speak Lord, for thy servant heareth."

The Fourth Call

> **And the Lord came, and stood, and called as at other times, Samuel, Samuel. Then Samuel answered, Speak; for thy servant heareth.**
>
> **And the Lord said to Samuel, Behold, I will do a thing in Israel, at which both the ears of every one that heareth it shall tingle.**
>
> **I Samuel 3:10-11**

The fourth time God called, it was different. This time, Samuel was prepared. He was ready to launch out in faith. The doubting and unbelieving period was over. He was ready to take God at His Word. He was ready to forget his feelings and launch out. When God called Samuel this time he said, "Speak Lord, for thy servant heareth." Samuel learned the principle of launching out. Many Christians called of God into full-time ministry are afraid to launch out. They are afraid of "how the water will look." They are not sure if they will fail or succeed. Many are afraid of failure and mistakes. If God called you, He will provide for you. He will not let you fail. He will not let your enemy laugh at you. Launch out, and not just "out there," but "into the deep." The deep is where the large fish are. God specializes in rescuing people from the deep. He specializes in impossibilities.

When you launch out into the deep by faith, God will create a new arena for you. God told Samuel, "I will do a new thing in Israel, at which both the ears of everyone that heareth it shall tingle." God will do a new thing with you and in you. The eyes that behold you will be astonished, and the ears that hear about you will tingle.

Because Samuel launched out in faith, God began to open his eyes of understanding. Samuel was never the same after this encounter. He never went to Eli again to ask if God was calling him or not. From that encounter, he knew how to hear and flow with God. He found out firsthand how to hear, discern and understand the voice of God.

Unclogged Pipes

> **And the Lord continued to appear in Shiloh, for the Lord revealed Himself to Samuel in Shiloh in the word of the Lord.**
>
> **I Samuel 3:21 AMP**

Now the baton was passed to Samuel and he became a great prophet in the land. The above Scripture shows us that the pipeline to God from Samuel was free from debris. Samuel's eyes were wide open and did not wax dim. As a result, the people of the land were blessed because it says, "the Lord continued to appear in Shiloh" and "revealed Himself to Samuel in Shiloh in the Word of the Lord." The

Lord began to flow freely again. The leader was blessed as well as the people.

The Potter's House

> **Arise, and go down to the potter's house, and there I will cause thee to hear my words.**
>
> **Then I went down to the potter's house, and, behold, he wrought a work on the wheels.**
>
> **And the vessel that he made of clay was marred in the hand of the potter: so he made it again another vessel, as seemed good to the potter to make it.**
>
> **Jeremiah 18:2-4**

For years, God's leaders have been marred. The Lord could easily have thrown them away like a cracked urn. But instead, He is remaking the flawed product into an entirely different vessel, "as seemed good to the potter to make it" (v 4).

The key point is that the marred vessel was not thrown away. Rather, the clay used to make it was crushed, soaked and returned in a shapeless but pliable mass to the potter's wheel. There, the work of shaping was begun all over again. This was repeated again, until the clay began to take the form that the potter desired. Through this process, God was showing Jeremiah what the Lord Himself would do with the nation of Israel. It is indicative of what God is doing with each of His leaders in this hour.

The crushing actually represents the love of God in action. The Divine Potter could easily have thrown the blemished vessels away. There are plenty of other vessels to work with. But, God's love demands that every effort be made to make this imperfect and unlovely form into what it ought to be, even if the improvement involves crushing it to bits so that it can be entirely remodeled. We must note here that the making of the vessel is not up to the vessel. It is up to the potter. Flexibility and trustful submission are all that the potter requires of the imperfect vessel.

The potter's eye is trained. No doubt, many would look at a flawed vessel and believe that it is perfect "as is." However, the potter, being an expert in such matters, is able to spot the hidden flaws and tiny hairline cracks that the untrained eye would miss. The potter realizes that the vessel is far from perfection. The potter also knows that the flaws are the kind that cannot be repaired easily. He knows at a glance that the vessel must be thoroughly crushed, and that the making process must begin anew.

When the potter is satisfied that the vessel has finally reached perfection, he will give the work his seal of approval saying, "It is finished." After this re-fashioning process, the finished product will be of use for God's plan and purpose. To be crushed by the hand of God is anything but a pleasant experience, but from God's point of view the crushing must take place to cause us to remain sighted leaders that can accomplish the purpose of God on the earth.

CHAPTER 8

THE RELEASE OF THE MORE SURE WORD

The leaders God is making and manufacturing in His factory are leaders who will consistently and reliably give the "more sure" word of the Lord.

> **And so we have the prophetic word made more sure, to which you do well to pay attention as to a lamp shining in a dark place, until the day dawns and the morning star arises in your hearts.**
>
> **II Peter 1:19 NASB**

Because of the importance of the accuracy of the word of the Lord, God is raising up men and women across the land with the "more sure" Word. Just as when Peter warned the Church at Asia Minor about false teachers invading the churches everywhere, these men and women of God will qualify the authenticity of God's Word. Peter knew the Scriptures were infallible. In the verse above, we see Peter declaring a certainty about the Scriptures. He said that they experienced a "more sure" word of prophecy. This declaration of Peter was backed by the apostolic witness of truth.

> **For we have not been telling you fairy tales when we explained to you the power of the Lord Jesus Christ and his coming again. My own eyes have seen his splendor and his glory:**
>
> **I was there on the holy mountain when he shone out with honor given him by God his Father; I heard that glorious, majestic voice calling down from heaven, saying, "This is my much-loved son; I am well pleased with him.**
>
> **II Peter 1:16-18 TLB**

The apostolic witness or testimony included not only hearing the Word, but also being an eyewitness of the Word. In the above Scripture, Peter bears witness that he "saw" the event (v. 16) and also heard "the voice of the Father." The leaders God is raising and manufacturing will have a firsthand experience with their manufacturer (God). They will understand the event of their making and will know how to hear the voice of God. Peter was making reference to the beautiful experience that took place on Mount Tabor, the "Mount of Transfiguration." The Mount of Transfiguration was, "the transformation place of Peter and a few of the disciples." They left the mountains totally transformed. They were transfigured by the power of God. The "more sure" word became real to them. This is what God is doing right now. He is taking His leaders to the Mount of Transfiguration and is making them all over again, so that they can be able to release the "more sure" Word of the Lord.

The Quality of an Apostolic Witness

The qualities of the apostolic witness are carefully drawn here. Peter weighed the issue of the word of prophecy and declared that there was still but a "more sure" prophecy. This word of the Lord has more legitimacy, more accuracy, and more validity. This word is more trustworthy. Why? Because Peter experienced the Word as well as a sense of verification (the apostolic witness). In various translations of the Bible, it is all recorded in similar form.

> **For we have not followed cunningly devised fables, when we made known unto you the power and coming of our Lord Jesus Christ, but were eyewitnesses of his majesty.**
>
> **II Peter 1:16**

This shows Peter and the rest of the apostles' sense of verification of the truth. Also, we see:

> **And this voice which came from heaven we heard, when we were with him in the holy mount.**
>
> **II Peter 1:18**
>
> **We [actually] heard this voice borne out of heaven, for we were together with Him on the holy mountain.**
>
> **II Peter 1:18 AMP**

And we ourselves heard this utterance made from heaven when we were with Him on the holy mountain.

II Peter 1:18 NASB

Because of the proof provided, both visual and audible, Peter was confident of the infallibility of God's Word. Because of the great encounter and processing in God's factory, the Mount of Transfiguration, the leaders that God is raising up in this hour will be confident of the infallibility of God's Word and the surety of it. They will flow in the spirit realm, because they have experienced the presence of the Lord.

Because of the importance of the "more sure" Word of God, God's leaders and people must know how God operates, and flow with Him. Waves of revival are characterized by powerful moves of God's Spirit in the lives of His people. Yet, even the most spectacular demonstration of God's Spirit will have to line up with the Word of God. Christians endanger their spiritual lives when they leave the Word of God to follow after spectacular manifestations. We should not be moved by signs and wonders that do not line up with the Word of God, no matter how spectacular they are!

Discerning the Right Voice

And he said, Go forth, and stand upon the mount before the Lord. And, behold, the Lord passed by, and a great and strong wind rent the mountains, and brake in pieces the rocks before the Lord; but the Lord was not in the wind: and after the wind an

earthquake; but the Lord was not in the earthquake:

And after the earthquake a fire; but the Lord was not in the fire: and after the fire a still small voice.

And it was so, when Elijah heard it, that he wrapped his face in his mantle, and went out, and stood in the entering in of the cave. And, behold, there came a voice unto him, and said, What doest thou here, Elijah?

I Kings 19:11-13

The rest of that verse says, ". . . the Lord was not in the wind. . ." After the wind, came an earthquake and a fire, but the Lord was not in the earthquake or in the fire. Verse 12 says, "after the fire a still small voice." After we have gone through the wind, the earthquake and fire of production, then God is ready to display, market and distribute to His wholesalers and retailers.

Certainly, there are times when God manifests Himself in spectacular signs and wonders. God could have been in the wind, the earthquake or the fire, as Elijah stood on that Mount in the wilderness. But, God chose to speak to Elijah in a still small voice. Elijah, His servant, recognized God's voice because he had been trained. God's leaders will learn to hear His voice and recognize the true move of His Spirit.

Now therefore send, and gather to me all Israel unto mount Carmel, and the prophets of Baal four hundred and fifty, and the prophets of the groves four hundred, which eat at Jezebel's table.

So Ahab sent unto all the children of Israel, and gathered the prophets together unto mount Carmel.

And Elijah came unto all the people, and said, How long halt ye between two opinions? if the Lord be God, follow him: but if Baal, then follow him. And the people answered him not a word.

Then said Elijah unto the people, I, even I only, remain a prophet of the Lord; but Baal's prophets are four hundred and fifty men.

Let them therefore give us two bullocks; and let them choose one bullock for themselves, and cut it in pieces, and lay it on wood, and put no fire under: and I will dress the other bullock, and lay it on wood, and put no fire under:

And call ye on the name of your gods, and I will call on the name of the Lord: and the God that answereth by fire, let him be God. And all the people answered and said, It is well spoken.

And Elijah said unto the prophets of Baal, Choose you one bullock for yourselves, and dress it first; for ye are many; and call on the name of your gods, but put no fire under.

And they took the bullock which was given them, and they dressed it, and called on the name of Baal from morning even until noon, saying, O Baal, hear us. But there was no voice, nor any that answered. And they leaped upon the altar which was made.

And it came to pass at noon, that Elijah mocked them, and said, Cry aloud: for he is a god; either he

is talking, or he is pursuing, or he is in a journey, or peradventure he sleepeth, and must be awaked.

And they cried aloud, and cut themselves after their manner with knives and lancets, till the blood gushed out upon them.

And it came to pass, when midday was past, and they prophesied until the time of the offering of the evening sacrifice, that there was neither voice, nor any to answer, nor any that regarded.

And Elijah said unto all the people, Come near unto me. And all the people came near unto him. And he repaired the altar of the Lord that was broken down.

And Elijah took twelve stones, according to the number of the tribes of the sons of Jacob, unto whom the Word of the Lord came, saying, Israel shall be thy name:

And with the stones he built an altar in the name of the Lord: and he made a trench about the altar, as great as would contain two measures of seed.

And he put the wood in order, and cut the bullock in pieces, and laid him on the wood, and said, Fill four barrels with water, and pour it on the burnt sacrifice, and on the wood.

And he said, Do it the second time. And they did it the second time. And he said, Do it the third time. And they did it the third time.

And the water ran round about the altar; and he filled the trench also with water.

> **And it came to pass at the time of the offering of the evening sacrifice, that Elijah the prophet came near, and said, Lord God of Abraham, Isaac, and of Israel, let it be known this day that thou art God in Israel, and that I am thy servant, and that I have done all these things at thy word.**
>
> **Hear me, O Lord, hear me, that this people may know that thou art the Lord God, and that thou hast turned their heart back again.**
>
> **Then the fire of the Lord fell, and consumed the burnt sacrifice, and the wood, and the stones, and the dust, and licked up the water that was in the trench.**
>
> **And when all the people saw it, they fell on their faces: and they said, The Lord, he is the God; the Lord, he is the God.**
>
> **I Kings 18:19-39**

I believe there are men and women who are experiencing this same apostolic witnessing. As God was aware of false prophets and false teachers invading the Church then, and He is well aware of it now. I believe that God is providing the "more sure" prophetic word in this hour, because of the prophetic anointing that hovers over this season.

God is ultimately concerned with the precision of His spoken Word. Therefore, He is imparting to His leaders and children a "clear" certainty. Yes, God is releasing divine words to His children with insurance policies attached, "more sure" prophetic words. I have witnessed lately certain individuals standing and declaring God's prophetic "now" word with a new boldness and confidence like never before. Surely, some of this came with time and training. But, if you were to hear their testimony and discern what is happening, you could see that they received a prophetic word with an attached insurance policy, a "more sure" prophetic word. Today, the apostolic testimony is making its way back into the Church. This is not to promote false apostles, but to provide empirical verification that the early apostles, like Peter and John, experienced.

And so we have the prophetic word made more sure.

II Peter 1:19a NASB

And we have the prophetic word [made] firmer still.

II Peter 1:19a AMP

Peter exhorts the Church that, because of this type of false prophet, false teacher and false thinking, the prophetic word of God needs to be more proven today. The Church must pay attention and take heed. Peter went on to say why this was important.

False Prophets and False Teachers

But false prophets also arose among the people, just as there will also be false teachers among you, who will secretly introduce destructive heresies, even denying the Master who bought them, bringing swift destruction upon themselves.

II Peter 2:1 NASB

Let's review the above Scripture very carefully and determine who these false prophets and false teachers are. Then, we must eradicate our own ill thoughts and change in these areas. I want you to focus upon the phrase, "the master who bought them," and the word "secretly."

First, we must reject the idea that these false prophets and false teachers are coming from the unsaved world. Peter is warning us that these individuals are somewhere in the Church, and that they have contact with you and I. That is how crucial this issue is. The Scripture says that they will be among you (meaning you and I) and they will secretly introduce destructive heresies. Notice the word "secretly" in the Scriptural passage in II Peter. These individuals will not introduce destructive heresies boldly, out in the open, obviously, or conspicuously. No, no, no! They are subtle, disguised and camouflaged. Their means of deception will go undetected, unless we heed Peter's warning and become developed in the area of receiving accurate words of the Lord, as well as receiving accurate, seasoned people as the oracles of these words.

To help us identify these individuals among us, Peter tells us that they deny "the Master who bought them." That means they are the born-again, tongue-talking, Holy Ghost-shouting Christians in the pulpits of our churches, and even in the pews beside us. Peter is talking about those who call Jesus "Master," those He bought with His blood.

Second, we must realize how closely we can interact with these individuals, and yet they will go undetected. That is why God is making and raising up leaders who will alert the Church of God about these people. In cities, towns, countries and nations, God is raising up leaders who will be prophetic, that is, able to hear the voice of God clearly and distinctively, and able to communicate it to God's people. A leader who has not been properly processed and manufactured by Him, will not be able to detect these spirits that have entered in their churches, groups and ministries. The leaders God is making will hear, see and demonstrate the power of God. Because of their sophisticated spiritual radar and antennae, they will be able to detect every moving object in the spirit realm that is not of God. They will also shoot down anything negative before it can cause damage to God's elect or God's work.

Let's look at this Scripture:

> **For if, after they have escaped the pollutions of the world through (the full, personal) knowledge of our Lord and Savior Jesus Christ, they again become entangled in them and are overcome, their last condition is worse [for them] than the first.**
>
> **For never to have obtained a (full, personal) knowledge of the way of righteousness would have been better for them than, having obtained [such knowledge], to turn back from the holy commandment which was (verbally) delivered to them.**
>
> **II Peter 2:20-21 AMP**

This is a picture of a veteran who has been in the church for years. The Scripture says that those with a full and -

*personal knowledge of Jesus! This disqualifies the babes in Christ! Let's be careful of those with titles and high positions. The Bible says that these individuals have the knowledge (present tense) of the way of righteousness, and yet, have again become entangled in the world's affairs and overcome by these things.

In other words, these are Church folk who were dipping, dabbing, slipping and sliding in the affairs of the world, while still in the Church. They neglected to cultivate their relationship with the Lord and were overcome by the world's foolishness. This group might include our friends, elders, ministers, even pastors, who have slipped, and are now "secretly" introducing destructive heresies. The question is, are you and I currently being exposed to false prophets and false teachers?

CHAPTER 9

UNDERSTANDING THE LEADERSHIP LEVEL

When we study the New Testament, we find out that God never sent an individual out alone. He sent out apostolic teams. Not because they were more righteous, but because they had more authority. They held a higher office than the priests over the area. The power of authority is something that the Church lacks wisdom in, but our earthly fathers had much insight on this subject. In the military order of things, a general outranks a colonel. They can be an ignorant, timid general, yet, they still outrank a colonel because of the office they hold.

In the Kingdom of God, princes only operate according to the measure of their authority. In the Bible, the story of Daniel explicitly sheds light on this subject. A righteous angel was held up for 21 days, while an archangel was in progress to set him free from the prince of Persia, simply because the demonic prince outranked him in authority. He certainly wasn't more righteous. That is why most men of God today, can still operate in sin, and yet excel in what they do, because most of them stand in the apostolic office. Their office covers them, not their private moral life.

They teach you in seminary that God does not use an unclean vessel. This is a lie. Just examine yourself and note some of your secret sins. Yet, God still uses you. This is an example of some of the old fairy tales that you are taught in the seminary. God will use anything, even a jackass. But God is not pleased if your vessel is unclean nor is He pleased with you operating in sin. If you don't understand this principle, you will have a hard time figuring out why one person can accomplish great exploits for God, even in sin, yet you can try the same strategy and fail. You pray, fast and tarry for weeks, maybe months. You can try to use every Scripture available, yet, you accomplish nothing. The reason is that one moves in an apostolic office while the other does not. This does not mean there is something wrong with you. You just have to find your measure of authority and abide in it. Once you find God's blueprint for your life, it will put an end to competition, jealousy, inferiority complexes, and strife, because you know what and who you are. That's wonderful! That's freedom!

God's Methods Versus Man's Method

There are a couple of important things that we must learn. We must know that God's methods are not programs, but men. Plus, it is not just any man, it is the right man. When God said in Ezekiel 22, "I sought for a man," that man may have other men with him. He may have a board of deacons and elders, and, he may have committees. But, God looks for "a man." When God gets His man, He does His job through him. Israel screamed for four hundred years in Egypt, asking God to release them from the bondage of Pharaoh.

God heard them. But, God waited on a man, and that man was Moses. But, even when Moses showed up on the scene, God waited eighty more years to use him. His ministry did not launch out overnight. The largest Christian magazines did not launch him. Christian television did not launch him. God did not even launch him immediately. God said, "No, not yet." "I'm going to wait until he is made."

The tragedy in the Charismatic Church is this; as soon as a man gets baptized in the Holy Spirit, or he evidences a power gift, a vocabulary gift, or is a great expounder of the Word, they are thrown immediately into the ministry. God's method is, He will hide a man for years. During this time, He breaks the man and puts His character into him. Because of this process, the man is able to stay married to the same woman and can endure every trial of ministry until the end. But if a man launches out before he has developed Godly character, he may acquire a measure of power that he cannot handle. Before you know it, that same man will fall flat on his face. The Church has a tendency of launching men too soon. We look at their abilities, talents and anointing, but they still must be proven. If you study the way God schools men, He never launches them early. He always uses the method of "hiddenness," until a man is "meet for the master's use." Sometimes we try to rush God. We say, "God, you better hurry up." But God is never in a hurry. We are the ones in a hurry.

When Lazarus died, Jesus took His time getting to Lazarus's tomb. There, He was confronted by one of Lazarus' sisters who scolded Him for being four days "late." To Jesus, He was four days on time.

The Jethro Principle

And it came to pass on the morrow, that Moses sat to judge the people: and the people stood by Moses from the morning unto the evening.

And when Moses' father-in-law saw all that he did to the people, he said, What is this thing that thou doest to the people? why sittest thou thyself alone, and all the people stand by thee from morning unto even?

And Moses said unto his father-in-law, Because the people come unto me to inquire of God:

When they have a matter, they come unto me; and I judge between one and another, and I do make them know the statutes of God, and his laws.

And Moses' father-in-law said unto him, The thing that thou doest is not good.

Thou wilt surely wear away, both thou, and this people that is with thee: for this thing is too heavy for thee; thou art not able to perform it thyself alone.

Hearken now unto my voice, I will give thee counsel, and God shall be with thee: Be thou for the people to God-ward, that thou mayest bring the causes unto God.

And thou shalt teach them ordinances and laws, and shalt show them the way wherein they must walk, and the work that they must do.

Moreover thou shalt provide out of all the people able men, such as fear God, men of truth, hating covetousness; and place such over them, to be rulers of thousands, and rulers of hundreds, rulers of fifties, and rulers of tens:

Exodus 18:13-21

In this scripture passage, we do not see the principle of plurality of governmental leadership, but finality of authority in one man. These men have real authority, real rule, but the hard cases come to Moses. This shows that it is not equality of authority. Every man in the Scripture does not have equal authority and equal vote. They all have a voice, they all have a say, they all have a measure of rule, but Moses had the final rule.

The most Christlike picture of the Kingdom of God is depicted in the story of David and the Davidic kingdom. Here we see David exercising plurality of leadership along with the principle of one man authority.

AND DAVID consulted with the captains of thousands and hundreds, and with every leader.

I Chronicles 13:1

Here, David is seen doing the same thing that Moses was instructed to do. We see an extension of the Jethro Principle in operation in the Davidic era.

> **Then Solomon spake unto all Israel, to the captains of thousands and of hundreds, and to the judges, and to every governor in all Israel, the chief of the fathers.**
>
> **II Chronicles 1:2**

Solomon, David's son, also in this Scripture is following in the footsteps of his father by appointing captains over thousands, and hundreds. Again and again, if you go through the Old Testament, you will find that these kings set up a government and a chain of command in the same way Moses did back in Exodus 18.

People of God, listen to me. My desire for you, as you read this book, is to discover who you are, and where you function in the Body as men and women of God. There are many leaders, with a Babylonian denominational structure, (which is not biblical), placed in positions in churches, ministries and groups, illegally. They have not been recognized nor approved by God. He did not place them in those positions. As a result, leaders are executing tasks that God Himself did not appoint them to do. A lot of leaders are in the wrong positions carrying the wrong burdens that God never placed upon them.

> **And be not conformed to this world: but be ye transformed by the renewing of your mind, that ye may prove what is that good, and acceptable, and perfect, will of God.**
>
> **For I say, through the grace given unto me, to every man that is among you, not to think of himself more**

highly than he ought to think; but to think soberly, according as God hath dealt to every man the measure of faith.

Romans 12:2-3

Before I can think soberly, I must go back and experience verse two which says, "Be not conformed to this world or this present age." This present age says that success, security, prominence and position are measured by the size of a thing. That *is* the world system. If I am not big, I am not good.

The World According to Madison Avenue

The world according to Madison Avenue holds that everybody is promoted according to their level of competence. In other words, you keep getting promoted until, finally, you cannot handle the job. Your church can be growing to the place where it begins to seem unsurmountable, and then you begin to have problems managing it. You may try to keep it a secret, in hopes that no one ever finds out the stress level you are experiencing. But, after a while you realize that you are drowning, because the problem is larger than your *grace* to bear it. That is bondage. It is not freedom. It causes astronomical amounts of stress and insecurity. As a result, a lot of leaders crack. If your ministry is killing you, you may consider two things:

1) you are not appropriating God's grace; or

2) you are taking something beyond your measure of authority, and God does not want you to have it. It will kill you.

Leaders are not called to meet every need. If you have a call of God, you have to stay within the circumference of that call. You don't go around trying to accomplish feats that are not included in your call. We have to find out where our gift and calling is, and we have to stay there. We have different measures in the grace of God. Many times we say, "Well, I have been to seminary longer," or "I have been in the ministry longer, so I deserve more." This is corporate thinking. There is no corporate ladder in the Kingdom of God. There is just the anointing upon whom He calls and then appoints, and whom he appoints, He anoints. "What if a denomination appoints me and God does not anoint?" It will never work. I will end up a mess. That is the world system and mentality. When God brings the right man, he may not have a degree from seminary, nor may he have your particular pedigrees of background. But, the minute he touches something dead, life comes on it.

God's Demand for Faithfulness

A denomination might say, "Well, you are faithful, you've paid your dues, and you've been here for a long time; but God says, "I don't know you." He says, "You are not my choice." If we do not understand this, we are going to find ourselves feeling jealous, striving, condemned and unworthy. We have to renew our minds and start remembering that God honors, in the Kingdom, faithfulness, and not positions. A faithful deacon gets as much honor as a faithful apostle. Because most Christians don't understand this, we strive to get out of being a deacon, so as to become an apostle. This is a great tragedy within the Body of Christ today. We cannot make ourselves into what we are not. It is God that makes a man.

There is a lot of talk about getting the pattern right. This is correct. But sticking *any* man into the right pattern will not work. It has to be the *right pattern and the right man.* If you do not use the correct combination, it will *never* work. God has a pattern for the Church, and if we do not use these gifted men, it will not work.

Characteristics of Levels of Leadership

Let's look, point by point, at the qualities and characteristics of these men.

The Captains of Tens

The captain of tens can have, probably, anywhere from fifteen to forty people. The New Testament application would be a home cell group leader or a home fellowship group leader. We view the captain of tens like this:

1) He is the father of an extended family. He is not the Father. He is the father of an extended part of another father's family. He does not have a public ministry. He deals with people primarily on a one-to-one basis, so he does not need

organizational skills. If that is you, that is your measure of rule.

2) He does not need a public teaching gift.

3) He knows Scripture, but he imparts it in a conversational way. He is not a preacher.

4) He is a lover of people. He loves to spend time with people. He loves to be with people. That is what makes him tick. He would be miserable any other place.

5) Small things matter to him. Did they send the birthday card? He is concerned whether or not flowers were sent to the sick woman in his home group.

6) He is an example to others regarding how to live the ordinary, everyday Christian life, on the job and at home. His main gift is obviously pastoral, but he is not a pastor.

7) He does not initiate strategy or vision. It never even occurs to him to ask where we are going. That is not his gift. There is nothing wrong with this person. He is concerned with people. But notice, he is a loyal follower of those who do initiate strategies and vision. His heart and mind is not to reason why, but to just do what he is being told.

8) He speaks positively, particularly of the leadership of the church, and puts that loyalty into the heart of the people.

9) He is an encourager. His life is characterized by joy and thankfulness. He is a beautiful person. This man should never pastor a church. He should never become a lead pastor. He must be a part of something bigger. So, another man fathers the Word, and he just gets a piece of it. He becomes the father of an extended family. To help is his gift. He is not a visionary. He is not a strategist. He does not recognize gift ministries. That is not his job. He is just a "one-to-one" guy with fifteen to forty people. Don't ever get him above that or he is gone.

Captains of Fifties

These are usually staff pastors, associate pastors, leaders, elders, senior pastors, deacons, etc. Let's review the captains of fifties:

1) This man can handle fifty to two hundred people. This includes the children and the women. He is still primarily a father of an extended family, but the family is a little larger.

2) He is a lover of people. They love him and people feel free to come to him. He does not have an answering machine. He always likes to be accessible to people.

3) He likes to be on a first-name basis with everybody. He feels badly if he cannot remember a name on Sunday. He wants to know everybody, and has time for them. That is what makes him tick.

4) He can teach publicly, as well as minister personally. That is where he begins to differ from the captains of tens. He has some limited organizational skills. He thinks of those kinds of things.

5) He is not going to have national impact, but he has a quality that touches ordinary people in ordinary ways. This kind of leadership is programmed to a limited size. He probably cannot grow to more than a hundred adults because they would not be able to get to him and when they cannot get to him, it bothers him.

6) His vision is for the local church only. His teachings are primarily upon practical Christian living and character, who we are in Christ Jesus.

7) He does not initiate strategy or vision, and if he is honest, he longs to be under somebody.

8) This person is insecure. He has to go to conference after conference, every four months. He has to get a fresh word and a new teaching, so that he can run home and hold up for another four months. Then he repeats the same pattern all over again. Why? Because he is not God's appointed to lead a church. He is not a man of vision. He is not a man of strategy. He desperately needs to be under someone.

9) He is not able to identify gifts and ministry in others, and so, he never brings it out as a blessing to the Body of Christ. Why? Because that is not his gift. He cannot

recognize it. He does not know how to release and develop leadership.

10) If he is not a secure man, men of greater gifts are a threat to him; particularly women, gifted women.

11) People of greater gifts love this person. But after a while, the leader gets frustrated and loses the people of greater gifts because the leader gets fearful and insecure. They spend sleepless nights saying to themselves, "These greater gifted people may take my ministry." "My congregation may like them better than me." "They are going to draw my members to themselves." After a while, the greater gifted people leave because of the flack given to them by leadership. Many ministries and leaders have lost people of such caliber because of this reason. But you shouldn't condemn them because they left. You do not really know why they left. They did not leave because they are rebellious people. They left because they are gifted people who need to have their gifts developed further. But, some leaders cannot discern the need. *They* may not even understand why they are leaving. But, again, it is not because they are rebellious people.

12) Without a relationship with greater gifted men in putting together a church, the church will just "gain a few and lose a few" year after year, without any significant, consistent growth. He must relate to greater gifted men, who can speak into his life and impart into his church. Such a church must be part of something larger or have no future. Sooner or later, the church will dwindle.

In the early days of the Church, the apostolic churches were linked with apostolic ministries under their authority, control, supervision and oversight. That authority and supervision covered them. The apostles broke open the nations because of their authority in the spirit realm.

Captains over a Hundred

A captain of a hundred can handle up to five hundred, but, he really shouldn't push beyond four hundred. Few of them can handle up to five hundred, successfully.

1) He has clear ability to teach publicly and to lead.

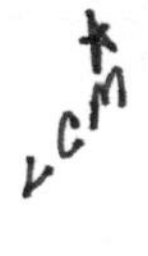

2) He can organize, unlike the captain of fifty. He delegates tasks, and knows how to release people to serve him. However, all he produces is servants. That is good, but not good enough. He only produces people who serve him. He does not produce people with real leadership abilities. They have no power to make decisions on their own. That is not real leadership. He can release people to serve and help him, but he does not release them to lead.

3) He is limited in his ability to initiate strategy or vision beyond anything local. His concern is primarily on his people, and he still wants to know everybody pretty much by name. He is a good man.

4) His primary gift is still pastoral. At times, he can be prophetic or evangelistic.

5) He often has a plurality of leadership, but they are merely helpers to him. He never releases them with any real authority. He cannot leave town without calling in several times. When he hears of something happening in the church that he did not know about, he becomes insecure and angry. His church work stagnates, because it has to come through him. One is limited to what one can handle, if he or she makes all of the decisions. You have to appoint the right man with real authority. This person is certainly going to be accountable. He or she can make those decisions without getting on the phone to someone else.

6) He cannot release gifts because he cannot recognize them.

7) He is a good man, but he can be easily intimidated. He is insecure and fights to keep things his own way. Greater gifted men and women are a threat to him.

Captains of Thousands

> **And he gave some, apostles; and some, prophets; and some, evangelists; and some, pastors and teachers;**
>
> **For the perfecting of the saints, for the work of the ministry, for the edifying of the body of Christ.**
>
> **Ephesians 4:11-12**

These are the Ephesians 4 ministries. They can handle from a thousand to a million, or more, it does not matter, because they are not going to do the work, anyway. They are going to equip others to do the work for them. Such a minister:

1) Has an effective public ministry to large crowds. He has to have the right voice and the right senses, to touch the crowd. In fact, a crowd turns him on. He is not frightened by the crowd. The bigger the crowd, the better. He may not do well among ten men or women in a group. But, before ten thousand, he will bring heaven down.

2) He draws people. He has to speak, and he speaks effectively. But, remember, God has to impart that to a minister.

3) He holds the people's attention and is known through his public ministry. He is able to share his heart, and do it in a transparent way, so people feel that they know him, even though they have never met him. Paul Cho, the pastor of the largest church, perhaps in the world, has not had his hands shaken by half of the people in his church, but they probably feel like they know him. Likewise with Ray McCauley of South Africa. He has a congregation of fourteen to fifteen thousand people. He also is aloof from his members because of the size. But, they also, probably feel like they know him.

4) He is a good organizer.

5) He knows how to handle and lead men.

6) Men of his gifts and abilities are drawn to him like a magnet, and they will leave the captains of fifties and

hundreds to follow him. Why? Because he has the ability to release their gifts and to bring them forth. That is why they are willing.

7) This minister releases all areas of responsibility and delegates the power to make decisions to others. He not only gives others authority, but power. But, he does make them accountable. He does not just give it and leave it. He always checks up and makes sure they are accountable. For example, if the music for the Sunday service is not flowing, he will make it his business to find out why.

8) He keeps his fingers on everything, but never gets involved with the details. That is not his job.

9) His primary concern is the vision for the house, strategy and hearing God's direction to lead His people. His concern is the work of the people. His concern is the work of the Kingdom and he will not spend the majority of his time with the daily affairs of his people. He is concerned about the people. He makes sure that they are cared for and well fed. But he, himself, will not be there.

10) His main concern is to spot leadership and gift ministries, and then develop and release them. He knows if he does not do that, his vision would not be fulfilled. He inspires gifted men and knows how to develop them, and he can cause them to go further in God with Him than they can go on their own. This is an important statement to note. Would you rather be chief of a little village? Or, would you rather be tenth in the mighty move of God?

11) He is more concerned to direct and organize the care of the people, than to do it himself on a one-to-one basis. He would do it one-to-one if he had to, but he will never undertake it alone. You will always see gifted men around him. An insecure man will always want to do it alone, even though he is a good man.

12) This man equips others for ministry.

13) A man that is a captain of a thousand can work submissively in a team with other men. He can submit to the headship of another captain of a thousand.

That's what happened in II Samuel 23 and I Chronicles 12. David's mighty men came to him. Now these were some bad dudes. One guy killed eight hundred men alone. They said, "We know God is with you David, so our hearts are with you." David asked, "Have you come to help me or betray me? If you came to further *your* career, don't come." But they said, "Our hearts are thine, O David." If you read about David's mighty men, all these guys are captains of thousands. They could have each pastored a church anywhere in the world. But they chose to be with David, because God chose David to establish the kingdom and they said, "We are dying to our vision to fulfill your vision."

> **And David said, Whosoever smiteth the Jebusites first shall be chief and captain. So Joab the son of Zeruiah went first up, and was chief.**
>
> **I Chronicles 11:6**

Joab was the commander-in-chief of David's whole army. He was the top man in David's administration. He was the only man that was not listed with David's mighty men. But, he is not on God's list of mighty men. This Scripture exposes one of David's "off" days. He was not being led by the Spirit. He was in the flesh. Joab was an opportunist, a professional, who was not motivated by heart servitude, but by burning ambition. He was willing to risk his life to get a name and a position. The other men came with a heart to serve David, even though they were mighty men on their own. Joab was a betrayer. He became a "thorn" in David's flesh. If we don't "flush" these Joabs out of our churches, we will never establish the Kingdom.

14) He is strong enough to bring correction to leaders, when necessary. He is not a wimp. He corrects leaders, when necessary. He does not allow disloyalty nor permit equality of authority.

15) He is secure enough not to have to be liked. This is what makes him a captain of thousands. These men are not made. They are born. You cannot send them to seminary. You cannot send them to leadership training. If they have it, they have it. If they don't, they don't. You cannot make a gift of men and women who are not called and ordained by God. All seminary and Bible school training can do is polish and improve what is already there. But, if you are not called, you are not called. There is no corporate ladder to climb in the Kingdom. That is the key.

16) The foundational years of these men and women are filled with growth pains, frustration and grief. You see, in the early years of their spiritual growth, they realize that they have a definite call and anointing upon their lives. So they cause grief to the captains of fifties and hundreds, because the captains may not be equipped to handle these rebellious young men and women who see so much more than they. They don't understand what is going on. The early years of these men are filled with anxiety and frustration. They must be released.

It is important to realize that when you choose a particular person for a task, assign them according to their several gifts and abilities. Don't give someone more than they can handle. If you cannot handle a thousand, do not try. You will find your congregation begin to dwindle down, down, down, because that is not your level of gifting. It's not that the people are rebelling. It's not that they are being taught incorrectly. The reason the congregation is dwindling is because you are trying to flow beyond your level. You are going to rise and fall to your own level of rule. Be very honest with yourself. You have to know what you are and what you are not. Then, your security comes out of that relationship.

CHAPTER 10

UNDERSTANDING THE LEADERSHIP TEAM

Hearken now unto my voice, I will give thee counsel, and God shall be with thee: Be thou for the people to God-ward, that thou mayest bring the causes unto God:

Exodus 18:19

I. What is the leadership team? It is church members who:

a. Stand out with quality lifestyles.

b. Are committed to the Word and to Jesus.

c. Are committed to the pastor and the church.

d. Are faithful in volunteer service.

e. Have a healthy family life.

f. Are willing to change and grow.

g. Are ready to give themselves wholly to the pastor and the congregation.

II. Your ministry will go no further than your ability to develop leaders.

And it came to pass on the morrow, that Moses sat to judge the people: and the people stood by Moses from the morning unto the evening.

And when Moses' father in law saw all that he did to the people, he said, What is this thing that thou doest to the people? why sittest thou thyself alone, and all the people stand by thee from morning unto even?

And Moses said unto his father in law, Because the people come unto me to inquire of God:

When they have a matter, they come unto me; and I judge between one and another, and I do make them know the statutes of God, and his laws.

And Moses' father in law said unto him, The thing that thou doest is not good.

Thou wilt surely wear away, both thou, and this people that is with thee: for this thing is too heavy for thee; thou art not able to perform it thyself alone.

Hearken now unto my voice, I will give thee counsel, and God shall be with thee: Be thou for the people to God-ward, that thou mayest bring the causes unto God:

And thou shalt teach them ordinances and laws, and shalt show them the way wherein they must walk, and the work that they must do.

Moreover thou shalt provide out of all the people able men, such as fear God, men of truth, hating covetousness; and place such over them, to be rulers of thousands, and rulers of hundreds, rulers of fifties, and rulers of tens:

And let them judge the people at all seasons: and it shall be, that every great matter they shall bring unto thee, but every small matter they shall judge: so shall it be easier for thyself, and they shall bear the burden with thee.

If thou shalt do this thing, and God command thee so, then thou shalt be able to endure, and all this people shall also go to their place in peace.

So Moses hearkened to the voice of his father in law, and did all that he had said.

And Moses chose able men out of all Israel, and made them heads over the people, rulers of thousands, rulers of hundreds, rulers of fifties, and rulers of tens.

And they judged the people at all seasons: the hard causes they brought unto Moses, but every small matter they judged themselves.

Exodus 18:13-26

a. Jesus developed three, then twelve, then seventy and then five hundred.

b. Leadership training is a lifestyle.

III. You must have faith for leaders to grow up from out of the body.

And when Abram heard that his brother was taken captive, he armed his trained servants, born in his own house, three hundred and eighteen, and pursued them unto Dan.

Genesis 14:14

Moreover thou shalt provide out of all the people able men, such as fear God, men of truth, hating covetousness; and place such over them, to be rulers of thousands, and rulers of hundreds, rulers of fifties, and rulers of tens:

Exodus 18:21

And he said, So is the kingdom of God, as if a man should cast seed into the ground;

Mark 4:26

a. Don't look for leaders from other places. Look for potential in those around you first.

1. Learn about people.
2. Learn to see ability.
3. The statues you need are inside the rocks. You need to "chisel" them out.

b. Pray in tongues for God's will for each leadership position.

Wherefore let him that speaketh in an unknown tongue pray that he may interpret.

For if I pray in an unknown tongue, my spirit prayeth, but my understanding is unfruitful.

What is it then? I will pray with the spirit, and I will pray with the understanding also: I will sing with the spirit, and I will sing with the understanding also.

I Corinthians 14:13-15

IV. Leadership training should be in all aspects of the church.

a. As new converts, start training them to help others.

b. Through ministry training opportunities build leaders.

1. Some will move up into full-time staff positions.

2. Others will stay as helpers.

c. Remember good people need training, not just teaching.

V. Believe in the people in your church.

Moreover there are workmen with thee in abundance, hewers and workers of stone and

timber, and all manner of cunning men for every manner of work.

I Chronicles 22:15

a. God has given you the best. Believe it.

b. Your belief in them will cause them to believe in themselves.

VI. Be committed to the people around you.

And as ye would that men should do to you, do ye also to them likewise.

Luke 6:31

a. You don't need a "position." You need a specific person.

b. The strength of your team is based on your commitment to them.

VII. Give people room to grow.

And he said, So is the kingdom of God, as if a man should cast seed into the ground;

And should sleep, and rise night and day, and the seed should spring and grow up, he knoweth not how.

For the earth bringeth forth fruit of herself; first the blade, then the ear, after that the full corn in the ear.

But when the fruit is brought forth, immediately he putteth in the sickle, because the harvest is come.

Mark 4:26-29

a. You don't need a person with all the experience. You need one who will grow.

b. Let them "blow it" a few times.

VIII. Give continual teaching and training that will motivate your leaders to be their best.

Train up a child in the way he should go: and when he is old, he will not depart from it.

Proverbs 22:6

a. Training is never complete.

b. Learn to motivate leaders individually and through groups.

IX. Be straightforward and speak clearly to people.

A double minded man is unstable in all his ways.

James 1:8

a. You can't follow someone who is not clear about his direction.

b. Don't make people assume what you mean.

X. Don't accept mediocrity.

a. People will go no further than you expect them to go.

b. Set your standards high.

XI. Work with personal problems or needs. Know what is happening.

And when Jesus was come into Peter's house, he saw his wife's mother laid, and sick of a fever.

And he touched her hand, and the fever left her: and she arose, and ministered unto them.

Matthew 8:14-15

a. Your leaders need to be strong in their family lives.

b. Include spouses on the team.

XII. Reward those who labor with you.

Let the elders that rule well be counted worthy of double honour, especially they who labour in the word and doctrine.

For the scripture saith, Thou shalt not muzzle the ox that treadeth out the corn. And, The labourer is worthy of his reward.

I Timothy 5:17-18

a. Help them prosper as you want to prosper.

b. Let them know you love them.

XIII. Ten Important Truths About A Leadership Team

a. God is the Author and Finisher of the ministry. *Hebrews 12:2.*

b. God is the first Source of all needs. *II Corinthians 3:5.*

c. This is a lifetime commitment. *John 10:11-13.*

d. Renewing the mind is never completed. *Romans 12:2.*

e. People, not functions, must be the focus of our energies. *Matthew 23:11-12.*

f. Every problem can be solved through openness and honesty. *James 5:16.*

g. Agreement and teamwork bring power. *Matthew 18:19-20.*

h. We lead through relationship, not position, authority or emotional control. *John 14:15.*

i. We are committed to increase. Maintenance ministry is not an option. *Mark 4:30-32; Acts 19:20.*

j. The Word of God is the truth. Everything that is contrary must change. *Matthew 5:18.*

CHAPTER 11

OVERCOMING LEADERSHIP LIMITATIONS AND BARRIERS

Whosoever believeth that Jesus is the Christ is born of God: and every one that loveth him that begat loveth him also that is begotten of him.

By this we know that we love the children of God, when we love God, and keep his commandments.

For this is the love of God, that we keep his commandments: and his commandments are not grievous.

For whatsoever is born of God overcometh the world: and this is the victory that overcometh the world, even our faith.

I John 5:1-4

How oft did they provoke him in the wilderness, and grieve him in the desert!

Yea, they turned back and tempted God, and limited the Holy One of Israel.

Psalm 78:40-41

Introduction:

* We all have blind spots and barriers to overcome.
* God wants us to remove all limitations.
* Here are five keys to overcoming weakness.

1. Be honest with yourself about where your ministry or business is, and what is not working.

Either make the tree good, and his fruit good; or else make the tree corrupt, and his fruit corrupt: for the tree is known by his fruit.

Matthew 12:33

He spake also this parable; A certain man had a fig tree planted in his vineyard; and he came and sought fruit thereon, and found none.

Then said he unto the dresser of his vineyard, Behold, these three years I come seeking fruit on this fig tree, and find none: cut it down; why cumbereth it the ground?

And he answering said unto him, Lord, let it alone this year also, till I shall dig about it, and dung it:

And if it bear fruit, well: and if not, then after that thou shalt cut it down.

Luke 13:6-9

And when they were come to the multitude, there came to him a certain man, kneeling down to him, and saying,

Lord, have mercy on my son: for he is a lunatic, and sore vexed: for ofttimes he falleth into the fire, and oft into the water.

And I brought him to thy disciples, and they could not cure him.

Then Jesus answered and said, O faithless and perverse generation, how long shall I be with you? how long shall I suffer you? bring him hither to me.

And Jesus rebuked the devil; and he departed out of him: and the child was cured from that very hour.

Then came the disciples to Jesus apart, and said, Why could not we cast him out?

Matthew 17:14-19

a. We all see through the eyes of faith, but we must take a reality check regularly.

b. True faith causes you to be moving ahead and making progress.

c. Denial, ignorance or wishful thinking keep you stagnant and ignorant of reality.

II. Be honest with yourself about your personal strengths and weaknesses as a leader.

I therefore, the prisoner of the Lord, beseech you that ye walk worthy of the vocation wherewith ye are called,

But unto every one of us is given grace according to the measure of the gift of Christ.

And he gave some, apostles; and some, prophets; and some, evangelists; and some, pastors and teachers;

Ephesians 4:1, 7, 11

For I say, through the grace given unto me, to every man that is among you, not to think of himself more highly than he ought to think; but to think soberly, according as God hath dealt to every man the measure of faith.

For as we have many members in one body, and all members have not the same office:

So we, being many, are one body in Christ, and every one members one of another.

Having then gifts differing according to the grace that is given to us, whether prophecy, let us prophesy according to the proportion of faith;

Romans 12:3-6

a. Know what you are gifted and graced to do.

b. There are many ways to build a great church or business. Use God's strength to do it.

c. Deal with your insecurities and images that keep you trying to look good, and deceiving yourself and others.

d. Deal with your laziness and lack of discipline.

1. Study and pray.
2. Diet and exercise.
3. Marriage and family relationships.
4. Staff, congregation and community relationships. *I Timothy 3:2, 4-5, 7.*

III. Build a team of leaders around you that will complement and support your strengths and weaknesses.

Moreover thou shalt provide out of all the people able men, such as fear God, men of truth, hating covetousness; and place such over them, to be rulers of thousands, and rulers of hundreds, rulers of fifties, and rulers of tens:

And let them judge the people at all seasons: and it shall be, that every great matter they shall bring unto thee, but every small matter they shall judge: so shall it be easier for thyself, and they shall bear the burden with thee.

If thou shalt do this thing, and God command thee so, then thou shalt be able to endure, and all this people shall also go to their place in peace.

Exodus 18:21-23

a. Don't gather a bunch of people who are just like you.

b. Don't look for people who will think like you and agree with everything you say.

c. Every championship was won by a team, not an individual.

Where no counsel is, the people fall: but in the multitude of counsellors there is safety.

Proverb 11:14

Through desire a man, having separated himself, seeketh and intermeddleth with all wisdom.

Proverb 18:1

d. The team is there to meet the various needs of the flock or customers that you cannot meet.

e. Build a team. Don't hire employees.

He that walketh with wise men shall be wise: but a companion of fools shall be destroyed.

Proverb 13:20

1. A team has comradeship and heart for each other. Employees are there for what they can get.

2. A team sacrifices for the good of the whole. An employee takes care of himself first.

3. A team makes all of the players look good. An employee makes sure he looks good.

IV. Seek God for creative ideas. Use your creative imagination to reach the people in your area, and draw them into the church.

And he saith unto them, Follow me, and I will make you fishers of men.

Matthew 4:19

a. Jesus witnessed to Nicodemus differently than the woman at the well, or the lepers, or the Syrophoenician woman, or the disciples.

b. Get creative to touch the specific character and needs of your community.

c. Don't be afraid to fail.

d. Don't be another church on the religious page of your city.

V. Outlast the devil and every other negative thing around you.

That ye be not slothful, but followers of them who through faith and patience inherit the promises.

Hebrews 6:12

For ye have need of patience, that, after ye have done the will of God, ye might receive the promise.

For yet a little while, and he that shall come will come, and will not tarry.

Now the just shall live by faith: but if any man draw back, my soul shall have no pleasure in him.

Hebrews 10:36-38

a. We are not in this for short-term success.

b. After we have done all, we stand until we receive the manifestation of the promises of God.

Wherefore take unto you the whole armour of God, that ye may be able to withstand in the evil day, and having done all, to stand.

Stand therefore, having your loins girt about with truth, and having on the breastplate of righteousness;

Ephesians 6:13-14

c. Don't let the desire for short-term gratification rob you of your long-term success.

Then believed they his words; they sang his praise.

They soon forgat his works; they waited not for his counsel:

But lusted exceedingly in the wilderness, and tempted God in the desert.

And he gave them their request; but sent leanness into their soul.

Psalm 106:12-15

CHAPTER 12

HOW TO GROW FROM ONE LEADERSHIP LEVEL TO ANOTHER

Seest thou a man diligent in his business? he shall stand before kings; he shall not stand before mean men.

Proverbs 22:29

Going from one leadership level to another starts with a desire to go beyond where you are in terms of success in your life. It is a challenge to improve, increase and expand in business and in every part of your life.

I. Your Personal Success Level

A. Have you mastered the level you are currently on?

1. Be so good at where you are, that you have to move beyond.

2. Are you excellent, excelling where you are in terms of your job, work, the customers that you have, the service

you give, the business you have right now?

B. Are you willing and ready to change?

1. Are you personally, internally ready to change? Any true growth demands change.

2. Be ready to change your attitudes, leadership style, priorities and schedule.

3. Be ready to change your communication skills and attitude. If you are not ready to change, then you had better get used to the level that you are on right now.

C. Are you ready for increased stress, pressure and responsibility?

1. If you don't want the pressure you have now, you are not close to being ready for the next level.

2. You will stagnate yourself because you don't want the added pressure that goes with the next level.

D. Do you have a clear vision of what the next level is?

1. Do you really know what it is?

2. Have you tracked it, studied it, analyzed it, and written it down?

3. Start by seeing the big picture, then focus on that next step that will move you closer to the big picture.

E. How will your family be affected if you increase?

1. Most of us think about growth and increase and assume that marriage and children will follow the dog like a tail.

2. Honestly evaluate how this will affect your family.

F. Do you have the character and integrity for increased finances and influence?

1. Godly principles won't work without character.

2. What is going to happen to your character when you are making two to four times what you are making now?

3. Do you have the integrity to handle more money?

G. Do you have the heart to pay that price?

II. Your Support Circle Success Level

A. Are you ready to release certain relationships to rise to the next level?

B. Does your staff or team that you work with have the same desire that you do?

1. If you are in a partnership, do your partners have the same vision and desire that you do?

2. Are they seeking and desiring increase?

C. Who is close to you that will speak truth to you, no matter what?

D. Who is your mentor or the one who has gone this way before?

E. Can your staff or team handle the added responsibility and the increase?

III. Your Product or Service Success Level

A. Do you have the systems for increase?

B. What clients or customers do you need at the next level?

C. What three things are hindering your rise?

    1. Ascertain, analyze, talk it through, walk it through. Then come up with three things that have to be overcome, in order for you to rise to the next level in your business.

CHAPTER 13

THE CHALLENGES OF SUCCESSFUL LEADERS

God has a very special and unique preparation for each one of His leaders. The making of that preparation is the final step, and it often comes during the height of your ministry. The Word of God contains examples of men and women who encountered numerous hurdles before their ministry was birthed and established. The purpose of this is to purify the leader. God will only use pure leaders, whose only motive for ministry is to be used for the glory of God and the salvation of souls.

During these challenges, God removes impure attitudes of bitterness, selfishness and covetousness from a leader's heart, and replaces them with pure love. Producing faithful men and women of God is the primary purpose of God's hurdles. These challenges and struggles can and do occur throughout a leader's life and ministry. Let's examine each of these challenges, and see how they are responsible in the development of a leader and his ministry.

The Time Challenge

The first hurdle is called the time challenge. This is when, according to outward appearance, God does not seem to be fulfilling the word he gave you in the past. This struggle will try your patience, and will force you to trust God to fulfill His call and ministry in His own time and way. This hurdle gives the leader an opportunity to grow in faith. It purifies a leader's motives and attitudes. During times of delay, a leader can see how his own impure, selfish or proud motives and attitudes can cloud his desires before the Lord. God desires transparent motives and attitudes in each of His leaders. It is during this period that God proves Himself to be a miracle-working, faithful God. He has called us to serve in His Kingdom. Many times, a leader believes that his own activity and striving can fulfill God's vision for His Church. Though God's leaders must cooperate with His plan, God always delights in using the weaknesses of men to give Him all of the glory.

> **NOW THE LORD had said unto Abram, Get thee out of thy country, and from thy kindred, and from thy father's house, unto a land that I will show thee:**
>
> **And I will make of thee a great nation, and I will bless thee, and make thy name great; and thou shalt be a blessing:**
>
> **And I will bless them that bless thee, and curse him that curseth thee: and in thee shall all families of the earth be blessed.**
>
> **So Abram departed, as the LORD had spoken unto him; and Lot went with him: and Abram was**

seventy and five years old when he departed out of Haran.

And Abram took Sarai his wife, and Lot his brother's son, and all their substance that they had gathered, and the souls that they had gotten in Haran; and they went forth to go into the land of Canaan; and into the land of Canaan they came.

And Abram passed through the land unto the place of Sichem, unto the plain of Moreh. And the Canaanite was then in the land.

And the LORD appeared unto Abram, and said, Unto thy seed will I give this land: and there builded he an altar unto the LORD, who appeared unto him.

And he removed from thence unto a mountain on the east of Beth-el, and pitched his tent, having Beth-el on the west, and Hai on the east: and there he builded an altar unto the LORD, and called upon the name of the LORD.

And Abram journeyed, going on still toward the south.

Genesis 12:1-9

The story of the patriarch, Abraham, beautifully portrays the time struggle. Abraham was 75 years old when God called him out of Haran to travel to Canaan. Being childless, the patriarch had made his home-born slave, Eleazar, to be his heir. But, God promised Abraham that he would have a child of his own. But, Abraham did not pass the time test. At the age of 86, he had an illegitimate son named Ishmael, through his concubine Hagar. Not until Abraham was 100 did God bring His promise to pass by giving him a son named Isaac. Abraham had to wait 25 years before he received God's promise of a son to be his heir.

The Motivational Challenge

Another challenge is the motivation hurdle. This is a heavenly "examination," in which God exposes to the leader what inner and outer forces influence his decision-making processes. God will arrange situations in order to reveal a leader's true intentions, thoughts, values and priorities that cause him to make choices or act in a certain way. The purpose of this is to disclose those inner drives and to purify them into desires for the glory of God, the salvation of souls and the edification of the Church. God puts you through the motivation struggle to expose unrighteous drives, and to replace them with motives of the Spirit, and true love out of a pure heart.

> **AND THE children of Israel set forward, and pitched in the plains of Moab on this side Jordan by Jericho.**
>
> **And Balak the son of Zippor saw all that Israel had done to the Amorites.**
>
> **And Moab was sore afraid of the people, because they were many: and Moab was distressed because of the children of Israel.**
>
> **And Moab said unto the elders of Midian, Now shall this company lick up all that are round about us, as the ox licketh up the grass of the field. And Balak**

the son of Zippor was king of the Moabites at that time.

He sent messengers therefore unto Balaam the son of Beor to Pethor, which is by the river of the land of the children of his people, to call him, saying, Behold, there is a people come out from Egypt: behold, they cover the face of the earth, and they abide over against me:

Come now therefore, I pray thee, curse me this people; for they are too mighty for me: peradventure I shall prevail, that we may smite them, and that I may drive them out of the land: for I wot that he whom thou blessest is blessed, and he whom thou cursest is cursed.

And the elders of Moab and the elders of Midian departed with the rewards of divination in their hand; and they came unto Balaam, and spake unto him the words of Balak.

And Balak sent yet again princes, more, and more honourable than they.

For I will promote thee unto very great honour, and I will do whatsoever thou sayest unto me: come therefore, I pray thee, curse me this people.

And God came unto Balaam at night, and said unto him, if the men come to call thee, rise up, and go with them; but yet the word which I shall say unto thee, that shalt thou do.

Numbers 22:1-7, 15, 17, 20

And he answered and said, Must I not take heed to speak that which the LORD hath put in my mouth?

But Balaam answered and said unto Balak, Told not I thee, saying, All that the LORD speaketh, that I must do?

Numbers 23:12, 26

The story of Balaam, the prophet, illustrates the motivation struggle in operation. Balak, the son of Zippor and the King of Moab, had seen how Israel defeated all of her enemies in the land. He feared they would destroy his nation, as well. Consequently, he offered to pay the prophet Balaam to curse the Israelites, to put an end to their victories. Balaam responded to Balak and said that the Lord told him not to go with the elders of Moab to curse the people of Israel.

Balak tried again, sending numerous and distinguished ambassadors to persuade Balaam otherwise. At the time, the Lord told Balaam to go with the elders of Moab and Midian, but to speak only the word the Lord gave him to speak. Balaam went to Balak, but each time he inquired of the Lord, the Lord told him to bless Israel. This greatly upset the Moabites and the Midianites. Through it all, God was exposing Balaam's motivation. Would he sell out, or would he be faithful to God's Word? God allowed Balak to tempt the prophet's motivation continually, and every time, the size of the bribe grew. Balaam's motivation did not stay pure. Though he initially tried to remain faithful in speaking only the Word of the Lord, the Lord allowed him to be tempted with much money, if he would only disobey God and curse God's people.

The Wilderness Struggle

The wilderness challenge is when God, directly or indirectly, guides a leader (or future leader) into a materially and or spiritually dry and desolate place. When no fruit seems to emanate from his life or ministry, a leader feels like he is in the wilderness. During such times, you wonder whether you really received a call of God upon your life. You appear to have no direct involvement in the true, living work of the Kingdom of God. Sometimes, a leader is left with no one else to talk to but God, Himself.

This struggle will cause you to increase your appreciation for the good things that God has already bestowed upon your life. God then teaches the leader how to discern whether the Lord, alone, sustains his spiritual life, or if he draws from his *own* ministry activity to sustain his relationship with God. God uses this struggle to strip the leader of all the wisdom and ways of the world, and to teach him the ways of His Spirit. Every leader must learn that God's ways are different from his own. Sometimes, the best way to learn this is through dry and lonely desert experience.

A dry land experience will cause a leader to acknowledge that his prayer life and study of the Word needs cultivating. Many leaders today need a dry place in order to exhaust the reservoir of sheer nervous energy that they draw from to serve the Lord. God desires His leaders to rest in Him; not strive for Him, in fear. The wilderness challenge will motivate a leader to seek the Lord through a consistent life of prayer and study of the Word. There, the leader will find the genuine and fruitful source of strength, God, Himself.

> **And it came to pass in those days, when Moses was grown, that he went out unto his brethren, and looked on their burdens: and he spied an Egyptian smiting an Hebrew, one of his brethren.**
>
> **And he looked this way and that way, and when he saw that there was no man, he slew the Egyptian, and hid him in the sand.**
>
> **Exodus 2:11-12**
>
> **Then fled Moses at this saying, and was a stranger in the land of Madian, where he begat two sons.**
>
> **And when forty years were expired, there appeared to him in the wilderness of mount Sina an angel of the Lord in a flame of fire in a bush.**
>
> **Acts 7:29-30**

Moses is an excellent example of someone going through the wilderness battle. Moses learned that his murder of an Egyptian (who he caught beating an Israelite) was made known to Pharaoh and the palace. He fled across the border to Madian for safety. There he married Zipporah, the daughter of a Midianite shepherd-priest, Jethro. She bore him two sons. The Bible lets us know in Acts 7:29-30, that forty years passed before an angel of the Lord called Moses to deliver God's people, Israel, from Egyptian slavery.

Why was this great man of God kept in the wilderness forty years, shepherding sheep, before God called him to his great prophetic ministry as Israel's deliverer and lawgiver? God took forty years to strip Moses of his Egyptian culture and prepare him for his work. Only then could Moses truly learn God's ways. This was the only means by which God could lead His chosen people out of the land of bondage.

In Egypt, Moses had probably mastered hieroglyphics and hieratic scripts, the reproduction of texts, letter writing, archery and other "civilized" arts. But, he probably did not learn much about the ways of God's Spirit. But after forty years in the desert, Moses learned what he needed to know to lead God's people out of Egypt.

The Battle of Being Misunderstood

The misunderstanding conflict occurs when those listening to a leader do not interpret correctly what is being said. People may misinterpret the true significance of his actions, words, attitudes or motives.

This challenge causes a leader to look for another avenue through which to communicate his feelings or views. It also causes him to examine his basic attitudes and motivations in communication. Many times, people will misunderstand what a person is trying to say, because the mode of communication may come across as harsh or stern.

In the New Testament, God was the one who opened the hearts of many people to believe the Word. A leader must trust the ministry of the Holy Spirit to quicken the truth of what he is communicating. God desires that every leader trust that His Word, through the Holy Spirit, will accomplish the task of building His Kingdom.

> **For consider him that endured such contradiction of sinners against himself, lest ye be wearied and faint in your minds.**
>
> **Hebrew 12:3**

A biblical term for misunderstanding is the word, "contradiction." Jesus is the prime example of the challenge of intentional and unintentional misunderstanding. He suffered this, not only from the Jewish people in general, but especially the Jewish religious rulers and even by His close followers.

The Patience Struggle

The patience struggle occurs when a leader's expectations of God are not fulfilled "on schedule." Patience is one of the fruits of the Holy Spirit. This word comes from a Latin word which means "to suffer." In the patience struggle, God challenges a leader to wait patiently or to endure some tribulation, without complaint. In portraying this quality, a leader calmly tolerates delay while refusing to be provoked by it.

To successfully pass through the patience struggle, a leader must yield his rights to Jesus Christ, in order that he will be able to wait for Him to do what He promised in His own timing.

The Vision Question

The vision challenge produces two questions: "Can you see the spiritual needs and answers of the people of God?" and "Can you resist opposition and adversity, and tenaciously hold the vision that God has given you as a leader?" This struggle actually shows a leader how shallow his spiritual insight really is. Many leaders are tempted to think that their present education, insight, knowledge and wisdom is totally sufficient to meet the challenges of Church life.

Many of their friends told them, "Oh, you will make such a good minister. You will really be able to do a lot for God, because you have so many talents and abilities." The school textbooks told them, "Now, this is the way to run a service; and this is the way to preach a sermon; and this is the way to save souls; and this is the way to cause the church to grow." But when they get into the ministry, they find that this is not so. They find that the true spiritual success of their ministries depends upon different criteria than what their friends or textbooks told them! What do they do now? They either drop out or desperately call upon God. Only the latter will make it.

The vision conflict ensures that the glory for success goes to God. A vision from the Lord may seem to die once, or even twice, so that its final fulfillment gives God much more glory than an uninterrupted march to success. God receives much glory when a vision is fulfilled supernaturally and in God's way.

THE WORDS of Nehemiah the son of Hachaliah. And it came to pass in the month Chisleu, in the twentieth year, as I was in Shushan the palace,

That Hanani, one of my brethren, came, he and certain men of Judah; and I asked them concerning the Jews that had escaped, which were left of the captivity, and concerning Jerusalem.

And they said unto me, The remnant that are left of thc captivity there in the province are in great affliction and reproach: the wall of Jerusalem also is broken down, and the gates thereof are burned with fire.

And it came to pass, when I heard these words, that I sat down and wept, and mourned certain days, and fasted, and prayed before the God of heaven,

And said, I beseech thee, O LORD God of heaven, the great and terrible God, that keepeth covenant and mercy for them that love him and observe his commandments:

Let thine ear now be attentive, and thine eyes open, that thou mayest hear the prayer of thy servant, which I pray before thee now, day and night, for the children of Israel thy servants, and confess the sins of the children of Israel, which we have sinned against thee: both I and my father's house have sinned.

We have dealt very corruptly against thee, and have not kept the commandments, nor the statutes, nor the judgments, which thou commandest thy servant Moses.

Remember, I beseech thee, the word that thou commandest thy servant Moses, saying, If ye transgress, I will scatter you abroad among the nations:

But if ye turn unto me, and keep my commandments, and do them; though there were of you cast out unto the uttermost part of the heaven, yet will I gather them from thence, and will bring them unto the place that I have chosen to set my name there.

Now these are thy servants and thy people, whom thou hast redeemed by thy great power, and by thy strong hand.

O Lord, I beseech thee, let now thine ear be attentive to the prayer of thy servant, and to the prayer of thy servants, who desire to fear thy name: and prosper, I pray thee, thy servant this day, and grant him mercy in the sight of this man. For I was the king's cupbearer.

Nehemiah 1:1-11

AND IT came to pass in the month Nisan, in the twentieth year of Artaxerxes the king, that wine was before him: and I took up the wine, and gave it unto the king. Now I had not been beforetime sad in his presence.

Wherefore the king said unto me, Why is this countenance sad, seeing thou art not sick? this is nothing else but sorrow of heart. Then I was very sore afraid,

And said unto the king, Let the king live for ever: why should not my countenance be sad, when the city, the place of my fathers' sepulchres, lieth waste, and the gates thereof are consumed with fire?

Then the king said unto me, For what dost thou make request? So I prayed to the God of heaven.

And I said unto the king, If it please the king, and if thy servant have found favor in thy sight, that thou wouldest send me unto Judah, unto the city of my fathers' sepulchres, that I may build it.

And the king said unto me, (the queen also sitting by him,) For how long shall thy journey be? and when wilt thou return? So it pleased the king to send me; and I set him a time.

Nehemiah 2:1-6

The story of Nehemiah's vision conflict and its fulfillment has two major elements. First, Nehemiah had spiritual eyes of faith to see the needs of God's people in Jerusalem after the Babylonian captivity. He knew that the Jews could not serve the Lord without their city, walls and temple being rebuilt. He desired God to use him to restore the ways that his people would use to worship God. He spiritually recognized that his people had sinned against God's law and had incurred God's judgment upon them. This should be the spiritual vision of every leader. We must recognize where the Church has sinned against God, and then *work* to regain God's blessing through repentance, faith and obedience to His Word. Secondly, Nehemiah's commitment to his spiritual vision from the Lord did not buckle under adverse circumstances.

So built we the wall; and all the wall was joined together unto the half thereof: for the people had a mind to work.

But it came to pass, that when Sanballat, and Tobiah, and the Arabians, and the Ammonites, and the Ashdodites, heard that the walls of Jerusalem were made up, and that the breaches began to be stopped, then they were very wroth.

And conspired all of them together to come and to fight against Jerusalem, and to hinder it.

Nevertheless we made our prayer unto our God, and set a watch against them day and night, because of them.

And Judah said, The strength of the bearers of burdens is decayed, and there is much rubbish; so that we are not able to build the wall.

Nehemiah 4:6-10

Nehemiah did not allow the enemies of Judah to discourage him in his vision. Instead, he gave himself to prayer. Similarly, every leader in this hour should never allow negative people or circumstances to cause him to lose the vision that God has given him for the church.

The Usage Challenge

The usage challenge is when a leader does not feel that he is "being used greatly." "Put it on the shelf," is a common description for this situation. God may put you "on the shelf" temporarily, for several reasons. The first reason is that God may desire to show the leader that he depends too heavily on his actual service or activity, rather than upon the Lord, Himself, for his joy and spiritual fulfillment. Being "on the shelf" may stimulate you to develop your personal prayer life and life in the Word more than ministry success.

This challenge also gives God the opportunity to purify the motives of His leaders. What causes a leader to act or speak the way he does? Why does he do the things that he does? This challenge may also deepen the message of the leader. Many leaders thrive on past sermons, instead of seeking the Lord for a fresh Word or experience. Some leaders stay so busy, they fail to take the time to study and sharpen their skill in the Word. But, the flock of God cannot constantly feed on the same sermons week after week without acquiring an appetite for more. At times, God will remove a ministry out of the public "eye" for a while, so that it will be motivated to deepen its understanding of the Word of God.

> **IN THOSE days came John the Baptist, preaching in the wilderness of Judaea,**
>
> **And saying, Repent ye: for the kingdom of heaven is at hand.**
>
> **For this is he that was spoken of by the prophet Esaias, saying, The voice of one crying in the**

wilderness, Prepare ye the way of the Lord, make his paths straight.

And the same John had his raiment of camel's hair, and a leathern girdle about his loins; and his meat was locusts and wild honey.

Then went out to him Jerusalem, and all Judaea, and all the region round about Jordan,

And were baptized of him in Jordan, confessing their sins.

Matthew 3:1-6

And the child grew, and waxed strong in spirit, and was in the deserts till the day of his showing unto Israel.

Luke 1:80

John the Baptist was born to Zacharias and Elizabeth. He was called to the prophetic ministry. It began in the wilderness of Judea. He was the forerunner of the Messiah, and the last and greatest member of the prophetic guild before the Kingdom of God was proclaimed. He was willing to accept a longer period of preparation. His length of time in the desert was longer than the duration of his actual ministry. Sometimes, a leader's ministry is so unique in its function, that God extends his preparation for reasons known only to Himself.

How many of us would complain if we had to spend thirty years in preparation for a three-and-a-half year ministry, as Jesus did? Most of us are so very service-minded, that we think we would be doing our best for God if we spent only three-and-a-half years in preparation for a thirty-year ministry. We must learn to accept God's full time of preparation for His ministry. The length of preparation differs for every leader. It will depend upon God's call on his life, his cooperation with the dealings of God and the future extent of his ministry. God must be trusted wholeheartedly in the fulfillment of all of the details of a leader's ministry, including the timing. John the Baptist was willing to be used of God only as long as God sovereignly intended to use him.

John the Baptist condemned Herod the tetrarch for the evil things he did, including marrying Herodias, his brother's wife. For this, Herod had him imprisoned and beheaded. What a humiliating death for one of the greatest eschatological prophets of all time. He had a short ministry, ending in decapitation. He was totally submitted to the will of God. He did not complain in prison about "being on the shelf," but submitted to God's timing for the end of his ministry.

People of God, let us determine, come what may, to be what God wants us to be in this end time move. Let us make a commitment to be steadfast, unmovable, always abounding in the work of the Lord. Humble yourselves and be made by the hand of God, that we might show forth His glory in our generation.

To request a complete catalog featuring books, video and audio tapes by Dr. John Tetsola, or to contact him for speaking engagements please write or call:

ECCLESIA WORD MINISTRIES INTERNATIONAL
P.O. Box 743
Bronx, New York 10462
Phone: (718) 904-8530
Fax: (718) 904-8107

Please visit our website at www.ecclesiaword.org or you may send an email to reformers@msn.com.